Looking for Something SERIOUS

Stories, Laughs, and Lessons from a Decade of Online Dating

LAUREN JOSEPHINE

♡
LJ

♡
LJ

Lauren Josephine

Looking for Something Serious

Editor | Emily Dickinson
Cover & Book Design | Kristy Twellmann Hill • umbrellasquared.com

Author's Note

This book contains truthful recollections of actual events in the author's life. The names of some individuals have been changed to respect their privacy.

For Grandma Jo
Knowing your love changed my whole life. Thank you.

♡ ♡ ♡

Preface

If you told me at age 22 that in the next decade I would go on well over 200 dates and have my heart broken approximately four and a half times, I'd bark out a hearty laugh and assure you that wasn't even possible. It was 2011 and dating apps weren't invented yet, so the idea of dating even 20 different people sounded like some sort of apocalyptic rom-com nightmare. *Two HUNDRED dates? What kind of psychopath goes on that many dates? Who has that kind of TIME?!*

Well, turns out, I did. For better or for worse, there was no magical future seer to come and warn me about my date-laden future, so I began my online search for love full of hopeful excitement. I felt boldly certain it would take me a year or two, at *max*, to find my soulmate. It seemed so straightforward: put up a few photos, type in a cheeky bio, add in some filters for the type of partner I was looking for, and violà! I was, of course, blissfully unaware of the mountain of consternation and uncomfortable growth that loomed ahead. Spoiler: it took a lot longer than one or two years max and there was very little "violà" involved.

Nearly a decade into my dating saga (after said mountain of consternation), I realized that my experiences and resulting feelings weren't actually all that unique. Everyone around me using dating apps was choking down different flavors of the same monotonous, maddening, and baffling experiences I was having. No one seemed to be immune. We were getting ghosted. We were getting love-bombed. We were getting whiplash from both happening within the same week. We were setting up second and third date plans only to have the person get unexplainably distant, disappear, but still watch our Instagram stories for the following year. We were having amazing dates (to us) only to receive the dreaded **"Sorry I didn't feel a spark"** text afterward. We were despair-deleting and desperation-re-downloading our dating apps on a bi-monthly cadence. Most modern daters have a collection of experiences like this, but so many of us feel alone. Like it *must* be about us. Like we must be wearing some invisible-to-us scrawl across our forehead that says, "BEST TO LOSE INTEREST IN ME IN 5–30 BUSINESS DAYS."

♡ ♡ ♡

Dating apps suck for almost everyone. But *why*? Well, I'd argue that online dating is a social experiment that we all just adopted without *really* understanding the ramifications. For millennia, humans found mates in the real world and then suddenly: Tinder. The idea of seeking love, partnership, and connection through a screen represents a monumental paradigm shift in the way we relate, but it snuck in rather unceremoniously; in the early 2010s, the on-demand app economy, which was just starting its illustrious boom, was quietly applied to finding human connection too. Tinder, the first "swipe" dating app, was launched in 2012, just after Uber, Postmates, and the Google Maps app. You can get everything else on the internet, so why not love too? It certainly made sense to me back in 2012 when I made my first OKCupid account, and it continued to make sense in 2014 when I downloaded Tinder, and in 2015 when I carefully crafted my three witty Hinge prompts. I ran blindly into the clutches of Big Dating with a hungry fervor. A new app? Three apps? Four? *Sure, I'll try it. The more the better!* I'm an early adopter type and I live in Silicon Valley—the "tech" epicenter of the world—so you better believe I'd be first in line for any app to find Love: The Thing I Wanted Most in the Entire World.

Those of us who were around before apps remember when meeting someone from the internet was unheard of at best, or a way to get kidnapped at worst. Yet here we are, a mere decade after the first dating app launched, meeting strangers from the internet voraciously, fearlessly, and maybe even more often than we meet people in "the wild." The sheer volume of people that we are able to meet and date now is on a scale that must be difficult for most of our born-and-raised-analog brains to comprehend. In the pre-app past, you might meet a few people a *year* you'd be interested in dating. Now you can easily swipe your way into multiple dates a week. You can download a dating app at 4 p.m. and have a date for 7 p.m. (quality not guaranteed). However, with the added volume of dates, there is naturally more...everything else. More rejection, more conversations, more remembering (and forgetting) details about people, more excitement, more disappointment, more highs, and more lows. I'm no sociologist, but I can only guess that we're not particularly well-equipped to deal with these drastically heightened levels of social interaction.

Regardless, this New World of Dating swept in like a convincing infomercial, promising the titillating opportunity to find love (or sex, or a validation pen pal) from the comfort of your home. But what about the longer-term implications of all of this for daters? How did quickly thumbing through digital stacks of potential romantic or sexual matches impact our psyches? How did trying to select a partner through six photos and a few canned prompts affect our ability to assess compatibility? Did access to so many more people actually improve our chances of finding a mate, like it seemed it should? No one really knew and no one really cared to know, at first. Because who has time to ask questions when you've got hot singles nearby waiting for *exactly* you?! And so, the foundation of dating began its tectonic shift underneath us *as* we were living it, and we barely noticed.

This book is about dating in Silicon Valley (mostly San Francisco) because it's where I dated, but more importantly, because it's a quintessential study of the marriage of tech and love. The area led the charge in applying tech solutions to *any and every* problem, want, or need. The eponymous Apple slogan said it best: "There's an app for that." As apps rose in popularity, convenience became king and as a result, in-person interactions fell away as the expendable second. These tech-first values naturally trickled down to the dating pool. And who, predominantly, made up that dating pool?

You guessed it: people in tech. People who'd flocked to Silicon Valley for high-paying, prestigious tech jobs at Google, Apple, or Facebook. Or people who took jobs at promising startups in some notable Series-letter funding stage, in hopes the startup would be a "unicorn" and eventually IPO to make the early employees millions. These people were predisposed to fueling an economy of convenience because they were otherwise busy chasing their dreams of striking it rich (and successful). Silicon Valley was the modern-day gold rush locale (think fewer gold pans and more tech-branded Patagonia vests) and it was the perfect petri dish for the growth and eventual takeover of the on-demand, convenience-first, human-second app dating culture.

So what does all of this actually mean for dating in Silicon Valley, on a tangible level? It means the dating pool self-selects for people who are go-getters, over-achievers, adrenaline junkies, big dreamers, and work-hard-play-hard-ers. It means good luck fitting in a date between someone's weekend ski trips, 12-hour work days, bi-weekly yoga classes, long Sunday hikes or bike rides, extensive South-East Asia travel schedule, and co-ed soccer league. It means success and busyness are often prioritized over mental health and personal growth, so you encounter a lot of 30- and 40-something Peter Pan types who look great on LinkedIn but severely lack relationship skills. It means that there is a pervasive sentiment of maximizing and always looking for the next exciting thing (or person). It means that the word "adventure" is egregiously overused on dating profiles and that a lot of those profiles look like humble-brag travel blog posts. It means you'll see a lot of CEOs, founders, and "entrepreneurs" on the apps, but always from some company you've never heard of. Oh, and how could I forget the software engineers? So many software engineers. (The show *Silicon Valley* is *eerily* accurate.)

What's more is that the expendability of in-person interaction has completely engulfed the dating culture here, so much so that meeting dating prospects in the real world has become an anomalous rarity. This trend isn't unique to this area, but it feels particularly exaggerated compared to other large cities like New York and Austin (where, at least anecdotally, casual flirting and approaches happen much more frequently). It's not uncommon in San Francisco to see people out at bars face-to-phone, or even swiping on dating apps rather than talking to the people around them. In other words, the art of the public approach feels like a nostalgic part of yesteryear. The single men and women here seem to be in a stalemate; single women dream of confident, attractive men approaching them but often give off "don't talk to me" energy when in public. Single men aren't approaching women for fear of coming off creepy or otherwise making women uncomfortable. And no one is making flirty eye contact unless they're at least four drinks deep. So dating apps have become a frustrating, near-necessity for people seeking any sort of romantic entanglement here (frustrating because no one is having a good time on the apps either).

Another important component of Silicon Valley dating is that people tend to "settle down" later (or not at all), so it's more common than not to be single into your 30s and beyond. On a positive note, this means it's relatively easy to get dates because the pool of unmarried people is abundant and always changing with new transplants. On the flip side, a dating pool full of late-settle-downers and questionably-permanent residents, compounded by the aforementioned I'm-busy-being-an-Instagrammable-Californian and next-best-thing attitudes, means getting into a committed relationship can feel like a Sisyphean task. Because it feels like you can only pick two of these:

1. Attractive
2. Has time for a relationship
3. Wants a relationship with you
4. Not moving away soon
5. Socially and emotionally competent

♡ ♡ ♡

So you might be wondering, is this just a book about a bunch of ridiculous Silicon Valley dating stories? Yes and no. Yes because *oh boy* there are some true characters in these pages (where else in the world would you see a bit.ly link to a "Partnership Vision" Google Doc on a dating app profile?!). But also no, because if my dating journey taught me anything, it's that when you stack a collection of dating stories together as a big messy pile, the sum is *so* much greater than the parts. There is somehow a rare wisdom that emerges from all the cluttered fragments of connection (even if that wisdom shows up impolitely late, long after you've already given up on dating for the third time). There is somehow a way that the whole mess reveals you (to yourself) and grows you (probably against your will). There is somehow a way that the very same experiences that break you, the very same people who left you wondering, and the very same nights that ended with you alone (again) eventually become precious fuel for your evolution. And it's almost always incidental; most people don't go into dating thinking, "This will be a great opportunity for personal growth! I will learn about my attachment issues! I can finally uncover the parts of myself that still need healing!" (If you do go into dating with that attitude, you are way more evolved than me.)

Dating apps, by their very nature, have this uncanny ability to trivialize dating into a series of transient, disposable, and forgettable encounters. But I'm here to present the antithesis: our dating experiences—even with people we'll never see again, even with people we never really "dated," even with people who ghosted after two dates—often have such meaningful impacts that we come out of our dating journeys completely transformed. We are relational beings and we weren't made to just date and forget, to form and sever bonds, to care and then suddenly not care, repeatedly, with different people, all within the same week, month, or year. Of *course* we struggle with dating like this. Of *course* we bend, break, and grow through this process. Of *course* we undergo a metamorphosis...it just might not be on *our* terms or timeline.

This is a book about unexpected transformation—the kind that sneaks up on you when you're busy trying to force your life to be what you always imagined it should be. It's a story about dating hundreds of guys from dating apps, not ending up with any of them, and discovering at the very end of it all, I had accidentally become the person I was meant to be. It's about finding purpose in the maddening liminal space, the space between no longer and not yet, when you wake up day after day wondering if you'll always feel this lonely (you won't). It's about how love will destroy you and build you and show you everything about yourself that you hide from. It's about learning to listen to your quiet insides even when the loud outside relentlessly tugs you away from yourself. It's about finding humor in the miscellaneous slice of humanity you'll experience when meeting strangers through your phone. It's about being open to the idea that the circuitous unknown will lead you to better places than you could have ever planned for.

There were so many times during my years of slogging through endless app dates that I sought out other people's dating stories in hopes that they would make mine feel a little more normal. Misery loves company, but also, misery needs hope. I wanted to read about others who went through the absolute dating ringer and came out happy in the end. I wanted to read about others who were convinced they'd end up alone and *did* get disappointed and hurt repeatedly but eventually found peace, or love, or both. The purpose of this book is to be that necessary dose of solidarity and hope for anyone who needs it. It's to validate anyone who has ever felt ashamed about how much they struggle with dating. It's to provide reflection, wisdom, and laughter about this crazy social experiment we're all in. Most of all, it's an invitation to trust yourself first and always, no matter what (or who) is happening on the outside.

Oh, and one more thing: I hope you'll take my word for it and avoid dating a CEO (especially in Silicon Valley).

I Wish We Could See Summary Statistics of Our (Love) Lives

I wish we could see counts of everything that's happened so far in our lives. Like, 547 Ritz crackers eaten. 88 jars of peanut butter consumed. 443 watched sunrises. 3 near-death experiences. 41 things lost, 12 of them returned. 10,006 minutes spent out of breath. 7 deep regrets. 19 sandwiches that were so good they changed your whole mood. 17 times you proclaimed, "This is the happiest I've ever been." 30 times you were convinced life was over for you and that you'd better just resign yourself to a lonely, broken future.

I wish even more that we could see summary statistics of our love lives. As if cataloging all of the chapters in a search for love would somehow make sense of it all. 103 first dates. 25 second dates. 16 third dates. 5 people who you loved; 4 who loved you back. 2 people who loved you and you didn't even know it. 3 times falling in love with the wrong person. 1 time falling in love again, with the same wrong person. 247 hours spent on dating apps. 6 times deleting the apps; 6 times re-downloading them. 11,455 texts sent to love interests. 9 times never hearing from someone again when you really thought you would. 15 times politely rejecting someone else. 2 gallons of tears cried, a third of those over one person. 3,442 days spent happy. 544 days spent completely and utterly heartbroken. 4 missed opportunities, when you walked right by someone who could have made your heart explode in colors you didn't know existed, but instead they remained forever unknown by you.

Seeing it all summed up would be strange and marvelous and heartbreaking, wouldn't it? It would remind you of the finite nature of our lives that is somehow both terrifying and relieving. And maybe, in the end, after reviewing it all, you'd realize that knowing doesn't change anything.

Maybe, in the end, it's the not knowing that makes our life so hauntingly poetic. It's the not knowing which love was unrequited. It's the not knowing which lost things (or people) will never return. It's the not knowing for sure what the sum is of anything in your life because it's the not knowing that compels that frustratingly insatiable urge to drag our weary legs out of bed each morning. To walk us into the new day, basket in hand, hungry to collect all of the moments, love, and sandwiches still out there for us to devour.

PART ONE

Insecure

(22–24 years old)

Qualifications for dating me: tall, brunette

CHAPTER ONE

The Roommate

The first of my questionable dating decisions started with Craigslist. It was summer 2011 and I was freshly 22, just out of college, and working my first ever nine-to-five job in Silicon Valley at a biotech startup. I was absolutely elated to start this new chapter because, unlike most people I knew, college had definitely *not* been The Best Years of My Life™. I attended UC Berkeley for bioengineering and I went in thinking it would be all: *Fun! Party! Hot, smart guys everywhere!* and it was more like: *Weekend studying! Calculus! Social awkwardness!* My hopes of meeting my future husband in college were quickly dashed when I realized that many of my male peers seemed to have little interest in even making eye contact with me. It might have been because of the whole "surrounded by awkward engineers" thing, but I read it as cruel indifference. As you do when you're about as secure as that old password you *know* you need to change. I felt hideous and so embarrassingly *average*.

These beliefs had taken root long before college though; I'd had a self-esteem problem, particularly with my appearance, for as long as I could remember. I was never sure why because, by all accounts, I'd grown up privileged with truly wonderful parents. But outside of academics, I never felt worthy. I was a precocious kid with a big heart who slowly morphed into a teenager with an overwhelming fear of being "forever alone." You know those small rejections that happen in adolescence that hold a disproportionately large amount of defining power in your sense of self? I had a full catalog and it seemed to me then to be Absolute Truth that Would Define My Romantic Life Forever.

In fifth grade, my childhood best friend and crush Alex told me no, he didn't want to be my boyfriend. In sixth grade, I miraculously got a Valentine from my new secret crush Jon, and then quickly found out it was my "friend" Cassie playing a prank on me. In seventh grade, an older boy told me I had a manly voice. In eighth grade, a friend played Cupid to get my crush Colin to ask me to the graduation dance, but then Colin's mom called me and told me he didn't actually want to go with me (mortifying). In sophomore year of high school, my first boyfriend left me for that same "friend" Cassie (Cassie sucked). In senior year of high school, my next boyfriend admitted he liked the way my best friend's stomach looked more than mine. On a high school graduation trip to France with my family, a street vendor guessed the dress sizes of my sisters and me as we were browsing his clothing: my sisters each were "small," and I was "large." All of these events cemented a simple, insidious belief inside me: I was not worthy of love. I'd carry this belief into my dating life for the next decade and it would cause me a lot of pain.

Anyway, back to Craigslist. My ultimate dream after my College Struggle Era was to live that sexy, unbridled 20s lifestyle that I'd grown up watching on TV: sharing a living space with roommates-turned-friends and basking in the rebellious, delicious freedom of being able to eat Cheez-Its for lunch or get tipsy on a Wednesday...all while actually having an income. I'd heard looking for housing shares on Craigslist was the best way to find this. A few weeks into my search, I excitedly came across a listing for an available room in a house of fun-loving 20-somethings.

I drove over on a sunny afternoon to interview for the room and immediately adored the house, with its lemon trees and quaint above-ground pool. The house came with four roommates—Jake and Jamie (a couple), Samantha, and Nico. Jake appeared to be the unofficial house ringleader and was clearly in sales. With a booming laugh and infectious confidence, he gave me a house tour and within a few minutes, I was already won over.

After the tour, we convened on the giant sectional couch and continued chatting. Nico sat in a corner of the couch watching a soccer game on his laptop and seemed only vaguely interested in interacting with me. *I wonder what his deal is.* Jake and Jamie quickly lassoed my attention back when they mentioned that the week prior, they'd played lobster soccer in the house. Jake pulled up a video and it was exactly what it sounded like: lobsters skittering across the kitchen floor, haphazardly jabbing at a miniature soccer ball with their rubber-banded claws. *How insane.* I wanted in. Lobsters, balls, and all. These were *exactly* the kind of shenanigans I was looking for.

Later that week I got a call from Jake with an invite to move in. *Yay!* My dad and my boyfriend at the time helped me move my smattering of IKEA furniture into my small room right next to Nico's. It took only a few days for me to realize Nico wasn't the cold, soccer-obsessed enigma of his first impression. In fact, I quite *liked* him. He was whip-smart—almost intimidatingly so. He was a software engineer working in tech (the first I'd encountered) and I was drawn to the way his brain worked. He seemed to have an answer for everything I asked him about. The fundamentals of day trading? The best sandwich shop nearby? Why the stoplights near our house were always out of sync? Check, check, check. We found ourselves pondering and ribbing each other mercilessly for hours.

Within a week, it hit me. *Oh god.* I was really attracted to Nico. *But no! I can't be attracted to him! I have a boyfriend!* This story would really paint me in a better light if I just decided to stay with my boyfriend and/or not get involved with my new roommate. But alas, I did neither: within a few weeks of moving in, I'd broken up with my boyfriend, skinny-dipped at midnight with all of the roommates after a drunken night out, and snuck into Nico's room one night on a cheeky dare from my best friend.

Who was this new me? Certainly not the devastatingly insecure girl who put all fraternity guys on a pedestal in college because she felt they were out of her league. Whoever this new, skinny-dipping-with-coeds Cool Girl was, it was working for me. Nico and I were quickly swept up in each other, blustery and reckless. We became a tangle of legs and lips at any hour of the day. *Whoever said you shouldn't date your roommate was dumb*, I decided defiantly. *It's so convenient!*

But it didn't take long for my naivete and underlying emotional unavailability to create inevitable fissures between Nico and me. In a moment of hasty reversal, I realized I had foolishly jumped right into a new relationship and started to pull away from Nico. I decided I should "date around" for a while. That's what people did, right? I had no idea, it just sounded somehow adult. I decided it would somehow be totally fine to start online dating while still living with Nico who, just a week prior, I was practically in a relationship with.

♡ ♡ ♡

Thus arrived the inaugural moment of my online dating career: creating my first ever online dating profile. Since it was 2011 (before dating apps), I used the website version of OKCupid. I spent a few months dating around, both online and offline. I dated a part-time model and a mixed-messages musician (more on these guys later) and both experiences went terribly. I came out of those months humbled with a bruised ego. I realized I was foolishly throwing away an opportunity to date this great guy right in front of me, even if he was my roommate. It was magnanimous of Nico to still be willing to give it a shot with me, because the backpedaling away from him to go date around was a glaring example of my unaddressed avoidant[1] tendencies that seemed to surface whenever someone "liked me too much." These tendencies, though usually dormant in the name of feeling anxious instead, would come back to haunt me multiple times over the next decade.

♡ ♡ ♡

About six months into living together, Nico and I became official. I wish I could say that our relationship was smooth sailing from there, but it most certainly was not. Despite my first bout of online dating going terribly, I'd been tainted by the possibilities of choice that I'd been flooded with on OKCupid. I subconsciously had one foot out the door in my new relationship and that soon became evident in my actions.

Shortly after we became an official couple, I planned to go to my first ever music festival, *Ultra*, in Miami with Jake, my best friend Jessiy, a couple other friends, and notably, *not* Nico (festivals weren't his thing). As we planned the trip, I realized I was going to be a fifth wheel. My discomfort about it started to burrow into my brain until I had an idea: I'd ask Nico for a hall pass![2] Just in case I wanted to make out with someone, of course. It seemed very reasonable and harmless

---

1   Throughout the book I'll make note of anxious and avoidant behavior, which is a reference to Attachment Theory. This theory, formulated by John Bowlby, posits that each person has a unique attachment style that influences how they act and feel in intimate relationships.

2   hall pass (noun): an agreement between a couple that one or both people can go outside of the relationship for sex or other physical "relations." Usually a bad sign, but you do you.

to my 23-year-old brain. (It was not reasonable and was actually a symptom of how terrified I was to be alone. I would only later understand how destructive it was to live in constant need of validation and attention from men.)

I was surprised when Nico met my request with extreme hostility. He questioned how I thought he'd *ever* be okay with that. I insisted that just kissing would be meaningless and that I was still dating *him,* after all. He eventually took an "I'm-not-okay-with-this-but-whatever" stance and told me to do what I wanted, since I'd already clearly made up my mind. I selfishly took this as a green light.

I didn't meet or kiss any strangers in Miami, but my request had served as a grenade nonetheless. A few days into my trip, Nico and I were catching up on the phone as I lounged on the warm Miami sand. He was acting strangely evasive and eventually asked a very unexpected question: what would I think if he'd had a threesome? I was confused. *Who in the world would he have a threesome with?* He quickly followed up and admitted he was using the threesome question to soften the blow of his real news: he slept with someone.

Um, what? Who did he even have time to meet in the approximately 72 hours since I'd left? My heart slammed against my ribs as I processed. Then it slowly dawned on me: Vicky. She was a new roommate who'd just moved in a couple of days before I left. *Another roommate? Was this Nico's kink?!* There was a very real possibility she didn't even know Nico and I were dating, but I was too shocked and livid to think rationally.

"VICKY?! YOU FUCKED OUR NEW ROOMMATE?!" I screamed at him, definitely in earshot of my friends and several strangers. Jake looked over at me wide-eyed.

Nico defensively countered that, well, he didn't know what I was *really* doing in Miami and *I* was the one who asked for the hall pass. I reiterated that my hall pass was to KISS someone, not sleep with them, but he was having none of it. (He had a point; my myopic have-my-cake-and-eat-it-too plan severely lacked empathy and didn't account for how Nico would realistically perceive my request.) We argued for a while and decided we weren't going to resolve anything over the phone. The whole festering mess would be waiting for me when I got home.

On the plane ride home, I marinated in emo music and stared despondently out of the window at the shifting landscapes below. I felt like that character in a movie who has just received *terrible* news and must *dramatically* ponder what to do next while Bon Iver plays moodily in the background. I chewed on the possibility that my entire life was imploding and it was at least 43% my fault.

I arrived home to chaos. Or more specifically, two *very* different versions of a story. Tucked into my nightstand was a note from Vicky—five pages, handwritten. She outlined all of the reasons that Nico was a womanizer and insisted that I should RUN, IMMEDIATELY. Nico insisted that Vicky came onto him and he just opportunistically took the opening. Aside from the polite roommate interview questions, I hadn't even spoken to Vicky. So, suffice to say, I had no idea if she was trustworthy. I had no idea if she even knew Nico and I were together, or what he told her. I had no idea what her motives were and I had no idea who or what to believe. I spent that first night home torrentially angry at Nico, trying to blunt the edges of my pain with cheap Pinot Noir. I'd never, ever been one to drink when I was upset, but I told myself this occasion justified it.

After that initial storm, forgiveness came quickly. I softened to Nico's side of the story. I knew the truth probably lay somewhere in the middle of the two stories, but I wasn't ready to lose a boyfriend to the words of a near-stranger, nor was I ready to face a breakup that I knew deep down I was the root cause of. So, I chose Nico. It felt convenient that I could justifiably resent him now, rather than dealing with whatever it was inside me that felt the need to ask for a hall pass in the first month of a new relationship.

Within 24 hours of my arriving home, Vicky decided to move out. A few days later as she was collecting her last items, she walked down the hall to Nico's room, darkening the doorway as she peered in at us—me on Nico's lap playing a video game with him, chummy as ever. (In hindsight, I feel terrible about Vicky's forced departure and I understand that she was probably pretty traumatized, but at the time I felt immaturely justified about the whole thing.)

"I'm leaving," she cut in abruptly. "The key is on the counter."

"Oh, okay, bye!" I said, too cheerily. The painful abbreviation of her tenure hung in the air. What do you say to someone who slept with your boyfriend but maybe she didn't know he was your boyfriend and maybe she was telling the truth but maybe she was also kind of unhinged but you didn't really have a way to know anything for certain? Yeah, I didn't know either. She lingered for an uncomfortably long moment after that, hotly radiating a glare that I imagine could have rivaled Medusa. Then she was gone and we never heard from her again.

After that, Nico and I dated for a year and a half (and remained roommates). I would have confidently told you then that I fully forgave him for the Vicky debacle and forgot about it after a few months, but I didn't *really* do either. It lingered inside my subconscious as a shameful reminder of my low self-worth (for staying with a guy who slept with the other roommate) and my moral shortcomings (for starting the whole thing by asking for a hall pass). I didn't have the tools then to dig up and heal the rot inside of me, so instead I began a crusade to cover it all up with external validation from men. Thus began an arduous, futile search for The One Man Who Would Finally Make Me Feel Worthy.

CHAPTER TWO

The Rooftop Serenader Who Insists We're Just Friends

Back to my first foray into online dating: I gingerly typed "okcupid.com" into my Safari window for the first time, unsure of how the whole thing worked. A brightly colored pink and blue homepage splashed across my screen with various phrases like, "The best free dating website" and "The Google of online dating." The impressive number of "online now" users, in the tens of thousands, was shown at the top left of the page.

I didn't need much convincing. I immediately created an account and began to fill out my profile. I uploaded a few of my favorite filtered selfies from the Photobooth app on my aging MacBook from college. In the written profile section, I showcased many of my important traits such as my profound comprehension of sarcasm and how I liked to be "out causing trouble" on Friday nights. I took a lot of time listing out my favorite TV shows, movies, music, and food because that's what I thought compatibility was back then. I'm sure I mentioned wanting someone "adventurous" who would be my "partner in crime." Finally, I set my height filter to 6' and above to complement my 5'9", set my distance radius to 25 miles, and answered at least 50 compatibility questions. Then I sat back, ready and waiting for my perfect man to be delivered to me from the internet.

My message inbox exploded. It was exciting at first, but then quickly tiring as I slogged through the ever-growing pile of messages, most of which did not interest me in the slightest. I received everything from odes about my "luscious breasts," to maybe-compliments like, "For a white girl you look like a decent rapper," to sweet messages from men I simply wasn't attracted to. Finally, I received a message that piqued my interest from a 25-year-old musician named Sean who vaguely resembled a Backstreet Boy.

On our first date, we discovered that we shared a love for the TV show *It's Always Sunny in Philadelphia* and really bonded over it. This shared "passion," combined with him being a really cute "older guy" who played guitar, solidified our compatibility in my mind. *We have the same sense of humor and we both love music, how awesome!*

On our second date, he took me to an upscale shopping area, Santana Row, where we ate dinner outdoors in a bustling courtyard. He brought his guitar and mentioned he wanted to play for me. *A guy playing guitar for little ol' me?!* I was very into it. I didn't know for certain but I optimistically suspected that cute guys only play guitar for cute girls they *like* like. At the end of our date, I blushed as he snapped open the buckles on his guitar case and pulled his guitar out to play for me, right in the courtyard, in front of all the bougie shoppers. A rom-com moment!

It turns out that being publicly serenaded was not as "rom-com cute" as I'd imagined. As he strummed and sang some sappy love song that he'd written for a recent album, I sat there uncomfortably, unsure of how to act. It was like those 10 to 15 grueling seconds when you're being sung happy birthday to, except it was several *minutes* and he was the opposite of my closest friends and family. *Do I just look at him smiling the whole time? Do I make eye contact with the passersby and smile in recognition that I am getting serenaded? Do I look down at the ground smiling? What do I do with my hands?!*

Finally, the song ended and I clapped sweetly with a huge grin, still unsure if I was acting the part right. He looked up proudly and I decided I was just being awkward (classic me) and that I should feel *lucky* to be serenaded like that. (Sidenote: I thankfully haven't been serenaded since and still don't know how to act, so please let me know if you have any tips.) Sean and I continued to go on dates, mostly planned around watching that week's episode of *It's Always Sunny*. We hadn't kissed yet, but our arms and legs had brushed against each other several times, so it felt like we were making progress.

One night, after several weeks of dates, I was telling him about how my house had a rooftop and my roommates and I were up there hanging out. He took the opening and suggested that the next time he came over, we should have wine and cheese on the rooftop, and he'd play guitar for me. Only the most romantic date idea ever! He *had* to kiss me then. Jake—who had quickly become my go-to for dating advice in the house—confidently convinced me that all signs were pointing toward Sean definitely trying to *hit that*. I was thrilled.

The rooftop serenade date came and went. He played multiple songs this time, all varying degrees of cutesy and John Mayer-esque. He even had a new chorus he was working on, that he'd written *for me*! But much to my chagrin, there was no kiss to go along with the very personalized serenade. I was starting to feel exasperated. *Am I reading this wrong?* I wrestled with my confusion for a few days before finally texting him and asking what was going on. His text back came quickly: **I'm feeling more of a platonic vibe here, but I really like you and I'd like to keep hanging out!**

Oof. I felt the red-hot shame of rejection prickle inside of me. I berated myself for reading the situation *so* wrong. But ever the Cool Girl, I swallowed my feelings and replied: **Sure! I'd love to keep hanging out as friends!** (I wanted nothing of the sort.)

Then came his drunk texts. We kept up a "friendship" for a couple of months and every weekend or two, he'd text me something flirty at some hour when I was either asleep or also drunk. I had not yet learned the joy of walking away from mixed messages, so I indulged him with replies and attention, desperately and secretly hoping he was having a change of heart about me.

I was sure I was right about said change of heart when he finally suggested a wine and movie night at my place one Friday evening. He came over with a bottle of red wine, which we shared in my bed while watching *Apollo 18*. About halfway through the movie and the whole way through the bottle of wine he grabbed my face and started making out with me.

Yes! It's happeninggg!

We rolled around, quickly forgetting all about the intense alien-massacre-on-the-moon situation on the screen. I felt a specific and compelling euphoria. I had gotten my first taste of the addictive nectar. That is, the sweet, sweet taste of enticing an unavailable man into wanting me. And my *god*, was it delicious!

But the high didn't last long—the following day he texted me telling me the previous night was a mistake and he didn't mean to cross a line. He still only wanted to be friends. I felt crushed and *so* embarrassed, but per the rules of being, like, totally chill, I let none of that show. He continued to bread-crumb me with flirty texts and I liked the attention so I let it happen. He eventually got a girlfriend, but he'd still text me periodically, and I could've sworn he was still flirting. Eventually, probably at the insistence of the girlfriend, the texts stopped coming.

I wish I could say I learned my lesson about mixed messages from cute internet strangers after this experience. But alas, rather than a lesson learned, this marked the start of an era.

CHAPTER THREE

The Part-Time Model with Just One Issue

"He was *flirting* with you."

My best friend Jessiy's elbow dug into my ribs as she pointed out what she thought was obvious. I surreptitiously glanced across the room at the incredibly attractive brunette guy that I had been painfully aware of since I arrived. We were staying in a cabin in Tahoe with my roommates and a bunch of their friends for a winter festival called *Snowglobe*. Most of the people there were strangers, but we'd all quickly warmed up to each other under the auspices of cheap beer and several games of Flip Cup.

The brunette was in the middle of a game of beer pong, flashing a smile that could woo binders full of women. He was the level of hot that actually made me a little resentful, because I was 100% certain he would never, ever give me the time of day. So, no, he was *not* flirting with me. I was sure of it. Guys always fell for Jessiy anyway, not me. She was care-free and effortlessly cool. I was insecure and try-hard, the type to get bent out of shape if I didn't fit in my 100 situps every day.

So...imagine my surprise when we were boarding the shuttles for the festival and the brunette chose the seat right next to me. *Must be a mistake, he just needed a place to sit.* It wasn't a mistake. He started talking to me and—dare I say—flirting with me! I was still suspended in disbelief that this guy was even talking to me, and heaven forbid I be presumptuous, so I acted a bit aloof.

A 30-minute shuttle ride and a whole vodka-and-Gatorade bottle later, he leaned in to kiss me. I was so oblivious that I cheeked[3] him. Jessiy chided me from the seat behind me and I reddened as I realized my grave mistake. *This hot-beyond-hot man tried to kiss me and I gave him my cheek. I am so awkward! I will never recover from this!*

Well, I did recover. Shortly after the cheek debacle, we kissed using our lips and became inseparable for the rest of the weekend. I felt like I was floating in a dream-come-true haze of euphoria (there's that high again). We traipsed through the festival arm-in-arm and spent the remaining hours at the cabin canoodling on any horizontal surface that would have us. The cabin was packed to the point of using sleeping bags on the floor for beds, so the brunette—who Jake had deemed "Model B" because he *was* actually a part-time model—and I kept it PG-rated.

---

3   cheek (verb): to give someone your cheek when they are very clearly going for your lips.

When Model B and I discovered that we lived in neighboring towns back in the Bay Area, he looked me in the eyes and told me he couldn't wait to take me on a date when we got back. I didn't know how to contain the excitement that was running amok like a wild toddler in my chest. *This can't be happening. He actually wants to date me?!* We said our goodbyes after the last day of *Snowglobe*, gushing out *I'll miss you's,* like we'd been dating for months rather than three alcohol-soaked days.

In the weeks following the festival, he actually did follow through and took me on several dates: sushi, TGI Fridays, a night of playing Settlers of Catan with his friends, and a sexy night of hot tubbing. At TGI Fridays, he gazed at me over a plate of curly fries, with that smile that could start wars, and purred, "I want to keep you around." I cemented that moment into my brain as clear evidence he was super into me. This would be important ammo to use against my anxiety later, whenever it struck.

Everything seemed to be following my fantasy timeline perfectly:

1. Meet outrageously hot guy
2. Hot guy magically takes interest in you out of a room (cabin) full of women
3. Hot guy takes you out on fun and sexy dates
4. Hot guy slowly but not that slowly falls in love with you because you're that irresistible

We were clearly on Step 3, and Step 4 seemed soon to follow. A couple of weeks into seeing each other, somewhere between Settlers of Catan and hot tubbing, we started sleeping together. This was way too early for my usual sex timeline of waiting months, but enter again, Cool Girl who wanted to keep this elusive hot man interested. During this time, he also vaguely mentioned that he "didn't believe in marriage" but I was so enamored with him that I spent exactly zero moments considering what that might mean about our compatibility (or lack thereof—I *definitely* wanted to get married and I hoped then it would happen by age 27, at the *latest*. Ha!). Not listening to someone when they told me who they were would become a theme in my dating career.

Back to the sex: there was one...issue. Sleeping together was maybe too generous of a description. We tried to, but he couldn't get things...working. At first, when he wasn't able to get or stay hard, it made sense to blame nerves. Or maybe alcohol. But it kept happening, variables notwithstanding. And to make matters worse, he didn't address it. At *all*. I had never encountered this before and had no idea how to react. *Was it me? But he'd given me so much praise? He said I was pretty?* Despite how self-conscious I was at the time, I at least had the wherewithal to deduce that it *probably* wasn't about me, which made it all the more perplexing. Unfortunately, high school Sex Ed didn't include a unit on How to Address Erectile Dysfunction Tactfully with a Part-Time Model When You're an Inexperienced, Insecure 23-Year-Old. So, I did the sensible thing: I didn't address it either! We just kept having confusing half-sex. *This is fine. It's really no problem! I'm totally good with it. What's a bit of soft dick when you have your dream man?* I was training for the mental gymnastics olympics.

After about a month of seeing each other, I got a random phone call from him. He told me we should stop seeing each other. He said we were looking for different things. *Wait, what?* I was not expecting this at *all*, especially when only a couple of weeks prior he'd crooned that he wanted to keep me around. After our clipped conversation, I hung up and fell over onto the couch sobbing. I'd been rejected by the hottest guy I'd ever dated. He slipped right through my fingers. I hated myself for reasons I couldn't really explain.

I called my best friend crying, and then for some odd reason, I called my dad. Still teary-eyed and sniffling, I told him the PG-13 version of the rejection. He read between the lines and gave me a piece of advice I would continue to ignore for years to come: *Lauren, you have to choose someone who chooses you. If that guy doesn't want to be with you, you don't want to be with him either.*

♡ ♡ ♡

In 2014 (many years later), I was living in a house with a different group of roommates-turned-friends and was getting to know a new female roommate who had just moved in from Craigslist (the most underrated friend-finder). We'd reached the point in our burgeoning friendship that included discussing previous hookups. I had mostly only been in relationships, so the Part-Time Model came up on my shortlist. At the mention of his first name and a couple of other demographics, we discovered that we had both slept with him all those years ago, consecutively! And we both experienced the same One

Issue. She mentioned that he wasn't looking for a relationship with her either, or at all. *Huh, so it really wasn't about me after all!*

I hadn't consciously been looking for closure about this, but it had come knocking for me. Maybe that's how it works sometimes, I considered. Maybe clarity just falls from the sky months or years later. Maybe I didn't have to worry so much about having it all figured out *right now.* Maybe I could trust that the future held the answers I was seeking, even if I hadn't yet asked the questions.

CHAPTER FOUR

The Still–Married Guy

It was October 2013, a few months after Nico and I had broken up. We had been fighting a lot and I finally pulled the plug. I immediately regretted it and tried to renege, but Nico insisted we stay broken up. It was especially messy because we still lived together (well, well, well, if it wasn't the consequences of my own brazen, conventional-wisdom-ignoring decisions). Instead of dealing with the grief of the breakup, I buried it inside and jumped right to furiously dating and partying. A lot. (I don't recommend this approach because, as I later learned, trying to skip your grief doesn't work. It'll just come back later with a vengeance. When Nico got a girlfriend a year later, I completely lost it and had to grieve him *then*.)

On this particular October Sunday, I was feeling a mixture of recklessness and FOMO[4]—the sort of mood that leads to hangovers and regret. So, I decided in a moment of peer pressure to tag along at the last minute to the second day of

---

4   FOMO (noun): fear of missing out. Made worse by social media. Made better by a really good couch.

a Halloween-themed music festival. At the pregame, I tossed my flimsy promise to myself to "just drink a little" straight into the trash. By the time the daylight started to fade, I was in a dusky, drunken daze at the main stage of the festival. The reverberating music vibrated through me as I swayed, packed into a sea of inebriated 20-somethings.

Being newly single, my usual M.O. would be to scan the perimeter for hotties and hope through some act of magic they'd notice me and come talk to me. But for once I was lost in the moment, savoring the crisp autumn air on my skin while dancing with my friends. So, I completely missed the ridiculously attractive tattooed guy dancing right in front of me.

The way we met felt like a dream, where the scene just starts in the middle. We were strangers and then at the behest of his friend who said something like, "You're both hot, you should make out," we were kissing. I hadn't even gotten a good look at him, so when we pulled away after making out for some indeterminate amount of time, I was shocked. *Holy shit*. He had smoldering brown eyes, a strong jawline, muscular shoulders, and was easily one of the most attractive men I'd ever interacted with. I was grateful for my insecurity-be-gone potion (alcohol) because I'd never have the guts to speak to him sober, let alone make out with him. We spent the rest of the night together, melding our friend groups and ruining any chance of a good Monday.

The following week, he took me on a date to a picturesque rock-climbing gym at the tip of San Francisco (where he lived) overlooking the Golden Gate Bridge. I didn't live in San

Francisco yet, so this date only added to his sexy "city guy" appeal. Shortly after arriving, I realized that in the light of day, sober, I could barely form sentences around him. I don't know if you've ever been so insecure that the mere presence of a hot person steals your words, but there I was, 24 and doing my best mannequin impression while limping around in pointy climbing shoes.

The second date wasn't much better in terms of sentence formation. We went to a trendy open-air market near my house in San Jose for dinner and drinks. I needed at least two and a half glasses of wine to garner an appropriate grasp of the English language around him, so I sneakily took rather large sips of my Cabernet. A short while into the date, the conversation of previous relationships came up and he, *very* casually, dropped this bomb on me: he was still married. Okay, but he was *separated*, he justified. They had been living apart for a year! They'd married for green-card reasons! Honestly even one of those justifications would have been enough for me. I barely flinched. I'd bagged a hottie; who cared about the minor speed bump of him getting *officially* divorced?

I swallowed that giant shard of incompatibility too easily, nearly forgetting all about it. After dinner, he asked if he could come over and spend the night because he was running a 5k in the morning near my house. I hadn't yet learned what "spending the night" was usually a euphemism for, so I said, "*Yeah, sure!*" It was way too early to sleep together anyway, I reasoned. *That wouldn't even be on the table!* Well, it was, and we did. Yet again, way too early for me to be comfortable but there were those rickety, easily-broken-for-a-guy boundaries again. I desperately didn't want to be a "prude." To make matters worse, I'd unintentionally upset Nico when he heard us at some point late into the night. I was absolutely *not* planning to bring a guy home, let alone hook up with him. I felt awful.

After that night, Still-Married Guy took a timeless classic post-sex approach: hot and cold with a splash of avoidance. He'd text me intermittently and we'd meet up for blurry nights out in San Francisco and smash our faces together in too-loud bars. I paraded him around my friends, but he never introduced me to his. Regardless, I was under the delusion that this was going somewhere, so every time he hinted at wanting to see me, I jumped at the opportunity. Desperation is a hell of a drug.

My close female friends had to bear the brunt of my ever-increasing anxiety about the situation. I spent hours ruminating to whoever would listen, picking apart each text (or lack of text) as if there was a secret code to be cracked that would get me closer to being his girlfriend. Never during this time did I even consider the whole "still married" thing— I'd swept it so far under the rug that I had completely forgotten about it. So when I eventually did volunteer that tidbit of information to my close friend Lena after months of "dating" him, she lost it.

"HE'S MARRIED?! This WHOLE time?! You owe me lunch!"

Click. She hung up on me. I was alienating my friends, but I still clung ferociously to the hope that they were wrong and he'd come around and realize I was girlfriend material. He never did come around, but he did get uncharacteristically possessive a couple of weeks later when I was staying at Lena's house over the weekend and said no thanks to his late-night booty call. **Have fun with your boy,** he texted, insinuating I was with some other guy and that was the reason I wouldn't let him pick me up at almost 1 a.m.

We petered out after that and despite his rather obvious fuckboy[5] behavior (and that he was still MARRIED), I felt quietly destroyed about the whole thing. I held this insidious belief that if I were more attractive, he'd want to make me his girlfriend. He was letting me go this easily because I just wasn't *enough*. I didn't yet understand that I actually held no power in convincing a man in his fuckboy era to magically change his ways. I didn't yet understand that I actually shouldn't be in the business of *convincing* anyone to want me, ever. I didn't yet understand that my wanting him so badly despite us clearly having different relationship goals was a special brand of torture I was choosing for myself.

Many months down the line, I heard through the grape-vine he was "back" with his wife. That was the last time I ignored a wife-sized "speed bump." At least the last time *knowingly.*

---

5 fuckboy (noun): a guy who definitely does not want anything serious but will say the right things to get into your pants. He's the king of mixed messages and "u up?" texts and will never commit to you.

CHAPTER FIVE

The Guy Who Avoided Me in College

Shortly after things with Still-Married Guy ended, I got back on the love horse (OKCupid). I was armed with some new, important criteria in my search: no mixed messages! Not married! Not *obviously* emotionally unavailable! I felt emboldened and full of that early-20s confidence that comes after you learn a few hard lessons and decide you're now a picture of maturity and wisdom. *I'm done messing around, I'm ready to meet my person now!*

One day I got a match and message that shook me: it was from my (*very* unrequited) college crush, Noah. I hadn't spoken to him since I was in school and frankly was surprised he'd ever want to associate with me again. Let me back up and explain:

In college, Noah and I had mutual friends and, during my junior year, we started showing up at the same parties more often. He had a hot-guy-that-might-not-know-he's-hot thing going on, and I was drawn to his goofy aloofness. I considered him to be out of my league, no question, but I admired him from afar and would casually chat with him when it was socially appropriate. As far as I knew, I gave no hints that I had a major crush on him.

During one particular Christmas party, I chatted with Noah more than I ever had before. We were all drinking, so I'm sure I was also acting a little flirtier than usual. Maybe a little clumsier too: I tipped over in a chair at one point—more from stupidly leaning back too far than being too drunk—but I digress. I felt good about the night overall—even proud of myself. I'd talked at length to my crush and hadn't even acted awkward!

Apparently, Noah came away with a very...different impression. A few weeks later, my best college guy-friend Jeremy was having another party and invited the usual crew, including Noah and me. Just before the party, Jeremy came to me and told me Noah had privately asked him if I was going to be at the upcoming party, and if so, he didn't want to come. *WHAT?!* Noah didn't offer any more details as to why and I *certainly* wasn't going to probe. I felt maybe the most mortified I'd ever been in my whole life.

You know those cringy events that your brain replays while in an anxiety spiral, as it tries to convince you that you're actually a gross monster and people hate you? Yeah, this event was the Title Track for those spirals. For years. It was a top-three worst nightmare come true: my authentic, slightly flirty self caused such repulsion in an attractive man that he actively avoided me. And I had no idea how or why, so I couldn't fix it. I just had to live with the belief that some part of me was repulsive to this guy, and therefore, somehow, probably, all men.

So, I was absolutely shocked when, many years later, I saw Noah's profile picture pop up in my OKCupid message inbox. I opened the message and found a flirty opening line, quickly surmising that he had no recollection of me (at least not over the computer screen). After a few quips back and forth, he asked me out for tacos. Now you may be wondering: Lauren, this guy's singular action made you feel like hot garbage for years, why would you ever spend more time with him? And that is a really great point! But at the time, the addictive validation of being asked out by a hot guy trumped all logic and self-preservation. Admittedly, I also wanted to see if he'd remember me in person, and maybe—just maybe— be reassured that it was all some big misunderstanding in college.

As I walked up to meet him outside of the hole-in-the-wall taco shop in San Francisco, I watched his face for any sign of recognition. None. *Alright, he doesn't remember me at all... cool, cool, cool.* We got to chatting and I let him make the connection that we went to college together.

"Ohh yeah, you look kinda familiar!" I lied, "I think we had mutual friends! The sailing team?" I watched his face again, waiting for recognition. None. But I refused to be the one to "remember" him when I apparently wasn't memorable to him at *all*. What would I say to him anyway? *Hey...so we actually did know each other! We flirted at a few parties and then you went out of your way to avoid me and it decimated my self-esteem for years! Anyway, how ARE you?!*

So, no, I played it coy and treated it like a normal date. Unlike college, I now mostly knew how to identify when a guy was flirting with me, and he definitely was. Unbeknownst to him, while he was cracking jokes and smiling at me, I was having a major internal revelation. *It was never that I was disgusting or ugly. He's flirting with me! He clearly thinks I am attractive enough to go on a date with.*

Deeper into the date, he revealed that he wasn't looking for anything serious right now but would love to keep taking me on dates. Something about that admission snapped me out of any remaining crush I had on him. We simply didn't want the same thing, and that was fine! It sounds so simple, but this was a ground-breaking realization for me—that a guy not wanting to be in a relationship with me didn't have to mean anything about my worth, nor did it have to mean he was a careless butthole. He wasn't a villain and I wasn't some grotesque undateable woman. We were just two people who would share a couple hours together and then (probably) never talk again. This realization felt like a healing salve to the wound I'd been carrying around since The Event in college.

I turned down his offer for more dates and we parted amicably. I never did get an answer as to why he was avoiding me at that party, but I didn't need to know anymore. I was starting to notice a trend about closure: it seemed to arrive in its own time, through its own door, and in a way you'd never expect.

How to Be a Cool Girl (and Lose Yourself)

"I should be fine with this."

For a large chunk of my dating career, this mantra ran through my head on a marquee—a bright, blinking reminder of who I was supposed to be. By my mid-20s, I was well-practiced in pretending.

The first time I heard of the Cool Girl was while reading the book Gone Girl, but I had been unknowingly idolizing this archetype long before there was a clever name for her:

The girl who is the perfect blend of feminine and sassy.

Playful, witty, and irreverent.

Confident and chill.

Hard-working, but also effortless.

The girl who dates easily and is not only palatable but irresistible. She sleeps around as she desires because she's not scared of anything, least of all a man losing interest after sex.

The Cool Girl seemed like the answer to all of my problems. She was an easy North Star to hitch my sad little wagon to; an identity to replace the one I'd deemed faulty inside of myself. Any time something felt off while dating, I reverted not to my own feelings, but to the flawlessly irreverent Cool Girl's:

Sex on the third date, way before I was ready? Sure!

He only expresses affection toward me when he's drunk? That's fine!

He's still married but promises they are separated? I'm okay with that!

He's terrible about following through but promises he's into me? I'm sure he's just busy!

Each rejection, each ending, each unreturned text was an opportunity to renew my valiant effort to not give a shit. But, like, in a cool way.

♡ ♡ ♡

You've probably been there—trying to embody an archetype to make yourself more "desirable." So often while dating, we get into the habit of trimming our corners and folding parts of ourselves away so that we can fit into a mold. We quiet parts of ourselves that we deem not suitable for public consumption. We pick apart our bodies in the mirror, promising ourselves that if we could just lose 10 pounds, then we'd be worthy. We tell ourselves that if we could just "chill out" a little more, everything would be fine. We lacquer over our real selves with a shiny ideal and then get frustrated when our humanness dares to seep through the cracks of our meticulously polished exterior.

And so, we enter the dating world as dimmed-down versions of ourselves; we go on dates and carefully navigate what and how much we show. We fear that if we let anything less than desirable be exposed, we'll eventually scare our dates away. We fear that we're too much, not enough, or somehow both at the same time. At the end of dates, we wonder desperately if our date liked us enough to ask us out again, rather than pausing to consider if we even liked them. After all, the Cool Girl wins everyone's affection, right? We agonize over how long to wait before texting them back, because a Cool Girl should always be busy (with yoga retreats in Bali, or going on spur-of-the-moment Monday dates, or being a girl boss, or whatever else we tell ourselves Cool Girls are doing).

We're embodying the Cool Girl as much as ever, yet nothing seems to stick. We get frustrated at the lack of connection. There's "just no chemistry," or we don't get a text back, or we become perpetually bored with everyone.

We start to wonder, "Is it me?"

Well, I have some good news and some bad news. Let's start with the bad news first: yes, it's you.

But now the good news: you have the power to change it.

All you have to do is stop trying to be the Cool Girl and start being yourself. Because in truth, the Cool Girl really isn't cool. The Cool Girl is a boring, generic version of you that has no zest, no courage, no originality, and no excitement. She has no controversial opinions and nothing uniquely captivating that makes her stand out. She's chill to the point of being bland and shallow.

Nope, the Cool Girl isn't cool at all. But you know what is cool? Authenticity. Vulnerability. Enthusiasm. Availability. Embracing and working on your flaws. Owning your truth no matter how scary it may be.

The Cool Girl is an embodiment that keeps us from forming real connections because, by being her, we hide and disown the very parts of ourselves that are the foundations for true intimacy. We worry that by bringing our complete, flawed, weird, emotional selves to the table, we will scare love away. But just the opposite is true. The more we own our imperfections and admit our truths— like the fact that sometimes on Sunday I cry for no reason and I always get barbecue sauce on my forehead when I eat ribs and actually can we not talk about work because I think our jobs are far from the most interesting things about us—the more opportunities we create to foster real, interesting relationships.

The Cool Girl isn't our fault, but she is our responsibility. We didn't create her, but we can make a pact to not be her. And in doing so—in uniting in an effort to ditch Cool Girl—we each create a little more space for the next girl to be as uncool as she damn well pleases.

PART TWO

Older but Not Wiser

(24–26 years old)

Qualifications for dating me: tall, brunette, seems
smarter than me, intimidating good looks, slightly
(but not completely!) emotionally unavailable

CHAPTER SIX

The Stanford Grad Student Who Never Showed Affection

Oooh, a Ph.D. candidate! I'd stumbled across the profile of a handsome, athletic grad student named Ryan who oozed that was-probably-in-a-fraternity-in-college charm. He was from the Midwest and getting a Ph.D. from Stanford in some impressive-sounding STEM[6] field—a classic Silicon Valley type. I considered myself somewhat of a sapiosexual[7] so despite our conversation that was only a small step above the conversations I'd had with chatbots, I decided to meet up with him.

In person, he was nothing like his dull messages. He was also devastatingly attractive, much more so than his pixelated pictures let on. I was immediately smitten, and—even better than smitten—intimidated. In other words, he was perfectly my type. (You may be wondering by now: how could *all* these guys be *so* attractive that you were intimidated by them? Well,

---

6   STEM (noun): an acronym for science, technology, engineering, and math.
7   sapiosexual (noun): a person who finds intelligence sexually attractive or arousing.

the answer is two-fold: first, my low self-worth led me to put most men I dated on a pedestal, hence my intimidation. Second, I had some lingering ugly-duck syndrome that led me to seek out the most attractive men I could find to prove to myself that *I* was attractive. I realized none of this at the time, of course.)

After an hour of bantering over Thai green curry, my cheeks hurt from smiling and Ryan said he'd love to take me out again. I felt like I was floating. *Finally! A guy who checks all the boxes and likes me too!* At the end of the date, he walked me across the parking lot and gave me a surprisingly stiff hug goodbye.

We continued to go on very G-rated dates for some time. About a month in, he invited me to an annual Beer Olympics event that his classmates were throwing. I cleared my weekend schedule and eagerly said, *"Yes! I'll be there!"* I was both excited and nervous; we hadn't kissed yet, but this seemed like the perfect opportunity. Because of the drinking, I knew I wouldn't want to drive, so I prayed for an invite to stay over.

On the Saturday of the event, I hemmed and hawed over my outfit choice. I *had* to present the right image when meeting his friends for the first time: a chill sporty girl who was also hot and surprisingly good at drinking games. I could *not* fuck this one up! (I know, I know, major Cool Girl vibes.) Upon arriving, I guessed I did well because his eyes lit up when he saw me.

"I told my mom about you," he admitted sweetly after we'd done friend introductions. *Swoon. This is definitely going somewhere!*

After a raucous afternoon of Beer Olympics that bled into the evening, he invited me to stay over. He warned me, however, that since he lived in the dorms, he only had a twin bed. I had no problem with this because, hopefully, it was one step closer to finally making out! But as the night progressed, we didn't seem any closer to kissing; dinner and a movie on his small couch came and went and we barely did more than graze thighs sitting next to each other. He eventually made the suggestion that we go to bed and my heart skipped a beat. *Okay, now, now is the time!* But as we shimmied into his tiny bed and lay straight-armed like un-touching sardines, I started to question everything. *Maybe he isn't into me? Maybe he's shy? Maybe I smell bad after a day of drinking games?!* Then, without notice, he said goodnight and turned his back to me to go to sleep. I didn't know it was possible to sleep in a twin bed with someone and not touch during the night, but that night I found out that it was indeed possible.

I woke up in the morning feeling dejected and confused, but he didn't seem phased. He greeted me cheerily upon waking up (still not touching me) and offered to cook me breakfast. I tried to shove down my utter bafflement and pretend like everything was fine. After breakfast, he walked me to the dorm stairwell and hugged me (stiffly) goodbye, mentioning he'd love to see me again soon. I plastered on a smile and thanked him for having me before bolting down the stairs and pulling out my phone to give my best friend the whole strange update.

We continued to date after that, for months. Polite dates; no moves on his part, crippling insecurity on my part.

Eventually one night, things turned a corner. We went out to The Patio—the local rowdy bar near Stanford—and got plastered. While on the sweaty dance floor, I felt an inkling of desire from him as we pressed into each other, our bodies sharing more surface area in those moments than they had over our whole relationship combined. Eventually, we both angled in for the kiss and lightly made out. *FINALLY!*

After that night, I had a renewed sense of confidence. *Okay he IS into me, it just took a while!* But outside of that blurry night, he continued to show me zero outward romantic or sexual interest on dates. I fell back into a distraught state of impotence. I felt nowhere near comfortable enough to ask Ryan about this, so instead I decided to try and recreate that night at The Patio. I organized a night out with friends and told him to bring his friends too. After we'd all had a few drinks, Ryan peeled off to go to the bathroom and I took the opportunity to interrogate his best friend Chase.

"Hey, can I ask you something? What's his deal? Why hasn't he made a move on me?"

Chase gave me a quizzical look as I probed deploringly; he had no idea what I meant. I explained how Ryan and I had been dating for months and he had barely kissed me. Chase barked out a surprised laugh of disbelief. He'd assumed Ryan and I had been sleeping together for months now. "NO, I WISH!" I exclaimed, exasperated. Desperate for an explanation, I even went so far as to ask Chase if Ryan was possibly gay (*sigh*, the only thing I could think of at the time). Chase didn't think so, which somehow only exasperated me more.

I was starting to lose it. I needed answers. At some point, Ryan's gentlemanly and not-overtly-sexual demeanor had crossed an invisible line from being refreshing to being maddening. I didn't know when or where that line was, I just knew that I went from *Ooh, he moves slow, love this!* to *Oh my god, touch me, please god, just literally anything, my fragile ego can't take this.* But I refused to go to the source (Ryan) to get answers because that would be just *so* cringe. So, I kept on, hoping each time we'd get drunk together that I'd inspire Ryan's affection. But it continued to not come reliably or repeatedly. I was getting my first taste of the dichotomy of many Silicon Valley guys—book-smart, successful, confident, but quite... perplexing in the romantic department.

Around five months into dating, we made a plan to meet up in San Francisco to go to a club after he went to another daytime party. On the afternoon of, we were texting about logistics for the night and I could tell he was getting drunker with each reply. Then the most surprising thing ever happened: he complimented my ass. I repeat: HE COMPLIMENTED MY ASS (via text, but STILL). In almost any other context, this sort of crude remark on my body would be "ew," but I was so starved for attention that I bathed in the pallid warmth of a "nice ass" text. I paused, hair half straightened, and stared at the text for a few minutes, making sure I wasn't reading into anything incorrectly. But there it was in plain text: him hitting on me. I replied back ultra flirtatiously and said I couldn't wait to see him.

But we never met up that night. He got too drunk at the other party and texted me saying he was sorry but he couldn't make it out. He went home to go to bed and all my excitement and hope deflated in a second. The momentum died after that night and though he texted me a few more times (not hitting on me) we never saw each other again. I never did get any answers, but I did see years later on Facebook that he got married. Maybe I should have asked more questions.

CHAPTER SEVEN

The Average–Looking Guy Who Nevertheless Tried to Make Me His Side–Piece

Ever the persister, I got back onto OKCupid and soon found a new match: Kurt. He looked like the typical San Francisco tech nerd (like, his company-branded Patagonia vest was a part of his personality), but from the beginning, he gave off the impression that he was very *in demand* with the ladies.

We went on a first date that was unmemorable except for the passionate kiss at the end. Almost none of my dates ended in a kiss, so I was caught off guard, mostly because it was a *really good* kiss. My lukewarm interest was suddenly dialed way up.

He was quite the texter, dishing out praise with practiced ease. I ate it right up. I was *starving* for praise after the six-month affection-desert with Stanford Ryan. Before asking me on a second date, Kurt noted that he was dating other women too. He used a metaphor to describe his dating life: it was like a meal with steak, potatoes, and other sides. Right now, I was his potatoes but he thought I could become his steak if I gave it some time. *Umm.* I'd never had a guy be this forward about dating others, and I definitely had never heard a guy compare his dating life to a hearty meal, so I didn't know how to react. But it sort of felt like a challenge and I wasn't one to say no to proving myself, so I agreed to keep seeing him. (Ugh.)

We went on a few dates and for some frustrating reason, his slightly-out-of-reach persona was pulling me in. I started to feel convinced that I really liked him. I started to lean on my girlfriends yet again, picking apart his texts, his actions, his aloofness. Without even realizing it, I found myself (yet again) attempting to nourish myself with breadcrumbs of attention from a guy. I spun around and around on a hamster wheel of exasperation until he eventually faded out. I mentally logged the whole experience as another example of me not being hot/interesting/sexy/alluring/skinny enough and begrudgingly moved on, dejected and confused.

Years later, he messaged me again on OKCupid. By that time, I'd grown enough self-esteem to see that I was never very attracted to him in the first place and that, at best, we were looking for different things. Or at worst, he'd use some weird pickup-artist methods on me to try and get me hooked. *Why did I get my undies in such a twist about this guy?!* I never replied.

CHAPTER EIGHT

The Low-Key Soulmate: Part I

For all the times I had been hurt, now it was my turn to be the villain in someone else's story. That's how this saga starts.

I didn't start off knowing I'd become a villain of course; we started as friends. Fast friends. I met him through Jake, my former roommate. I was hanging out at Jake's house one day when his new roommate walked in, carrying a funny-looking glass beaker apparatus. He worked in the aerospace industry, he explained, and this was a scrap part. He thought it looked cool so he decided to keep it; maybe put a plant in it.

"I'm Miles," he said with a friendly smile, plopping down next to me on the couch so I could examine his strange new piece of glass. I was also one to find particular joy in disposed-of oddities, so I was intrigued. Mostly by him. *Who is this curious, kinda quiet cute guy who sees interesting uses for old lab parts?*

After meeting that day, Miles and I continued getting to know each other through Facebook Messenger. We met right before I left for Oktoberfest in Europe, so as I gallivanted around Munich with friends, I felt a springy excitement whenever I'd hear the familiar *ping!* from my phone. Even with the nine-hour time difference, we found treasured, overlapping pockets of time to cram in hundreds of messages to each other.

Two months later I was daring him to kiss me in a dark, reverberating club in San Francisco. I could tell he really liked me and I was seduced by his restraint.

"Why haven't you made a move on me?" I asked between beats of heavy music.

He answered me with a kiss, and our plot thickened.

Over the next few months, Miles began to grow stronger feelings for me but I didn't know what I wanted. We became a dance of magnetic poles—him always wanting to be close and me slightly repelling him. I wanted him close, but not *that* close. When we were alone, I'd catch him staring at me with shameless adoration and it made me feel naked. Exposed. He seemed to love the parts of myself I was ashamed of, like how my face looked without penciled-in eyebrows or the way I always spilled *so* many crumbs when I ate. I wanted his attention, but I felt uncomfortable when he gave me too much of it.

We bowled forwards anyway, directionless and mismatched in our desires. We spent nights pressed up against each other in my full-size bed, physically close but nowhere near a label. I liked being around him but I wasn't enamored by him enough to date him. My avoidance was in full bloom; I thought I wanted someone who was super into me, but when I had that right in front of me, I wanted nothing to do with it.

I'd later pick apart these months together, trying to under-stand why love I didn't have to work for felt so...wrong. I hated how pathetic and anxious I felt when pining after unattain-able men, but something about it was familiar enough to convince me it was the way love should be. Freely-offered love felt cheap, a too-easily-won consolation prize. Love you had to strive for, to win, to scale treacherous mountains and cross deep valleys for, that was the love that made sense to me. It would take me many, many years to unlearn this.

♡ ♡ ♡

I think I love you, Miles confessed one night over text, after we'd known each other about five months. I looked at the text with a furrowed brow.

Wait what? Are you drunk? I replied, confused. He was drunk, but he meant it.

We continued further into our situationship[8] after that, him trying to shove down his feelings, me getting the ick[9] for unexplained reasons. I felt uncomfortable about the feel-ings-mismatch and started to put some distance between us. I explained to him that I enjoyed spending time with him a

---

8   situationship (noun): I was going to define this myself but this definition from Urban Dictionary really says it all—when one or two motherfuckers take part in a relationship, but out of fear of making things serious or messy, do not label it, leading to said relationship, ironically, becoming more serious and messier.

9   the ick (noun): When your attraction to a current or potential partner is suddenly flipped to a feeling of disgust. Usually for a small or odd reason, like the way they put on a shirt, or the way they eat a granola bar.

lot and didn't want to give that up, but I also didn't want to hurt him. So, in a classic situationship move, we agreed on some murky, ineffectual boundaries that made us both feel like we were doing the "right" thing, but didn't require much change in our behavior. Putting "distance" between us meant we spent marginally less time together but for much of it, we still acted like we were in a pseudo-relationship; we frolicked at music festivals together, we slept in the same tent while camping, we shared a bed during weekend Tahoe cabin trips, and we even took a romantic road trip down the California coast. (Mixed messages much? I was becoming what I used to hate.)

I hadn't been dating anyone else when I suggested some distance, but that soon changed. At the beginning of the summer, I met someone at a friend's house party and started going on dates with him (more on him in the next chapter). In an effort to not rub it in Miles's face, I kept my burgeoning relationship under wraps. I didn't know how to tell him without hurting him, so I omitted any clues I was dating someone new...until the night I brought my new almost-boyfriend to a birthday party at a nightclub that Miles also attended. The club was dark, crowded, and sweaty inside so I naively figured I could keep a reasonable distance from Miles and therefore keep my new relationship a secret. You can probably guess how that worked out.

A couple of hours and several drinks into the night, I ended up making out with my new boyfriend on the dance floor. I was blissfully drunk and not thinking about who might see me. Unbeknownst to me then, Miles (obviously) saw it. He was devastated; that was the first indication he had that I was dating someone else. He promptly left the club. His night had been completely ruined. (I found this all out later.)

After this, Miles wanted nothing to do with me. I'd shattered his heart. I hadn't meant to, but I just felt an alluring instant attraction to my new boyfriend that I'd never felt with Miles. I promptly sauntered into the sunset with this shiny new boyfriend, cementing myself as the calloused villain in Miles's life for almost a year.

CHAPTER NINE

The Good-on-Paper Guy with Six-Pack Abs

It was June 2015 and I felt on top of the world. I was 25 and finally experiencing fleeting bouts of real confidence. The confidence was mostly based on how I'd succeeded in bullying my body into a low body-fat percentage, as I'd recently taken to obsessively working out and tracking my food intake. It was addictive. I loved the feeling of control it gave me, over this body that always felt too "big." I loved the way my obliques would show when I would run three miles and then lift weights for an hour (or two) after not eating breakfast. I loved the way I could punish myself by eating 1,000 calories on Monday and Tuesday to offset my binge drinking and eating on the weekend. I was in the exact right mental space to fall in love with someone who was wrong for me.

"Hi, I don't think we've met before," I said, smiling warmly at the tanned stranger standing across the kitchen at a house party. He was a new face to me. This was unusual; at this point, I'd had the same large friend group for a few years and

I mostly saw the same people at parties, so I had long since let go of the hope of meeting a guy through my friends.

His name was Andrew and he was a college friend of the party host. Soon after my approach, I learned he was a software engineer and moving to San Francisco soon for a job (where I had recently moved as well). My ears perked up when he told me this. *Ooo, I wonder if he's single.* I couldn't help the thought; no matter how hard I tried to be chill, some relentless part of me was always—*always*—scanning.

Andrew and I spent most of the party exchanging grins and flirting. As the evening wore on, we stood closer and closer together and I began to playfully hit his arm when he'd make stupid jokes. We developed an inside joke about milk. We discovered our shared love for soccer and other forms of fitness. Him, CrossFit, and me, rock climbing and weight lifting. I wasn't drinking that night but was feeling uncharacteristically confident. *I think he's into me!* I was right.

I had not planned on a late night, so I peeled off from the party early to go to bed as the rest of the party crew headed out to dance. On the way out, the party host stopped me and told me *someone* really wanted me to come out and dance. I stood firm on my decision to go home, but I could barely hide my excitement and told him to give Andrew my number.

Two-and-a-half grueling days later, Andrew texted me. He referenced our inside joke (*so cute*) and asked me on a rock-climbing date. After that, he asked me on a second date—dinner at an upscale Mexican restaurant. Then a third date to a major league soccer game. On our fourth date, he suggested we go to Lululemon, then get Chipotle and have a

picnic at Dolores Park (we both loved Lululemon and Chipotle—
it was clearly a match made in heaven). The only caveat, he
said, was that he had an apartment showing in the middle
of the day. He asked if I wanted to go with him to the showing.
He wants me to be present for a major life decision? So romantic!

From there, we glided upwards on what felt like a perfectly linear dating progression. First, integrating into each
others' social lives: I began introducing him to all my friends,
which was easy because he already knew a few of them. He
didn't have many friends besides his roommate, but that
didn't bother me! I had enough for the both of us. Second,
the romance: we kissed for the first time about a month in,
the first time we got tipsy together. Third, that indulgent era
when love begins to blossom but neither of you dare admit
it: we spent lazy, sun-kissed afternoons in the park together,
my fingers tracing the ridges and valleys of muscle on his
stomach and my mind wondering how I got so damn lucky.

We started spending nights together. Then whole, luxurious weekends. Our Saturday ritual became walking
hand-in-hand from his house to Whole Foods, filling our
basket with too-expensive produce, eating an impolite number
of cheese samples, and carrying our groceries back home to
cook a healthy (usually Paleo) dinner together. Sunday morning always came too quickly but we spent it slowly, warm and
folded into his white sheets. It was almost three months until
we finally slept together, partially because I felt awkward
and partially because he didn't bring it up. (I had ricocheted
in the other direction from the too-soon sex of my past, to
the point where I felt almost disconnected from my sexuality.

I had subconsciously learned that sex came with emotional pain.)

Once we cleared the sex hurdle, everything continued falling into place like a dream. A month or so later, as we lay in my bed together under my twinkle lights, he was looking at me in a peculiar way. I asked him about it. "I'm looking at you because I love you," he answered softly. My hand flew to my mouth. *Did he mean to say that?* He hadn't planned to say it then, but it slipped out and he meant it. I said it back. I love you. I love you. I love you.

I'd always heard that saying, "When you know, you know," and I finally understood. I *knew.* He was everything I'd always wanted: smart, playful, fit, brunette, and slightly mysterious in a way that made me feel inextricably and irrevocably attracted to him. Our lifestyles felt perfectly aligned. I could take those foggy morning walks with him forever, savoring the way he'd offer his stomach as a sanctuary for my cold hands. I could spend night after night with him into eternity, chopping sweet potatoes and tickling his ribs as he cooked. It soon became impossible for me to separate him from my vision of the future. I began to build a home inside of him. A swift and sturdy construction, the type I had never bothered to build inside myself.

It felt like he was all-in too, so when he mentioned many months in that he had a hard time letting people in, I brushed it off. "What do you mean you don't let people in?" I asked him, confused, as I sat tucked in his lap. "It sure seems like you're letting me in." He answered in a tone of somber reticence, explaining vaguely that he'd always had trouble staying close to people. I tugged at his shirt, pulling him closer to me, as if to disprove what he was telling me. *I'm different,* I assured myself. *He's changing for me, I can feel it. He loves me.* In actuality, he was hinting at his emotional unavailability, but instead of seeing this as a warning sign, I saw it as a familiar invitation to work harder for his love.

We started talking about moving in together. During one of those early conversations, he mentioned that he only wanted to move in with someone if he felt sure he wanted to marry them. Before me, he'd been in a six-year relationship and they'd lived together. Near the end, she gave him a marriage ultimatum and he chose to end the relationship and move out. He didn't want to go through that again. Did that mean, I asked him, that if he was talking about moving in with me, he felt sure about...marrying me? He answered me with a smile and a nod and my heart exploded. *It's happening, it's real, it's everything I ever dreamed of!*

We started looking at apartments and my impending joy intensified. Every sun-lit living room, every kitchen counter, and every bedroom with a city view became fodder for my burgeoning fantasy future with him. Eventually, we found it: the most amazing apartment. It was on the top floor with abundant light flooding in from the bay windows and a spacious kitchen for us to cook in together. I clapped my hands together, elated. "This is it!" He agreed and we put in our application.

We didn't get it. I was devastated but determined to keep looking. But as I sent him more potential apartments, I began feeling an unexplained resistance from him. His criteria became more and more strict. He wanted it to be within walking distance of his CrossFit gym, and Whole Foods, and the train station. He wanted it in a specific neighborhood. He wanted a top floor, a big backyard, parking, a washer and dryer, and a big kitchen, in a narrow price range. The combination of all of these criteria made it near-impossible to find anything in the hyper-competitive San Francisco rental market. I felt frustrated and stuck but I refused to give up. *This is just a little hurdle, we can overcome it together.*

During this time, he started spending more and more time at his CrossFit gym. I couldn't understand what he was doing at the gym for over three hours, but I wasn't one to question him about his favorite hobby. He was also texting his female gym coach a lot, but they were friends and I fully trusted him so I thought nothing of it. He started to feel more distant than usual and I started to feel tiny nudges of wanting...more. I hadn't thought about Low-Key Soulmate for a long time, but I started to remember our connection and how my soul didn't feel that same vibrance when I was with Andrew. I started to notice how the conversations with Andrew often fell flat. I'd want to wonder and ponder and joke with him but my open-ended questions kept hitting dead-ends. *Was it always like this? No, no, couldn't have been.* I pushed away those nudges in the name of the picture-perfect future I was already married to.

Finally, after seeing yet another apartment that he turned down, I asked him, imploringly, what was going on. He admitted sheepishly that he didn't actually feel ready to move in with me. *Wait, what?!* I felt like I'd been hit by a bus, and rightfully so; it was the beginning of the end (even though I refused to see it then). We moved forward as if everything was going to be fine.

The next month brought on the series of events that would be the end of us. First, my grandma (who I was very close to) had been undergoing chemo for a brain tumor and I got the news that her condition was worsening. I asked Andrew to drive the hour and a half home with me to visit her in the hospital. He balked, saying he didn't really have time and didn't want to miss days at the gym. I was shocked and shaken by his flagrant disregard for something *so* important to me. I realized something was very wrong between us but this only made me hold onto him harder.

Sometime after that, we went on an attempted relationship-reinvigorating double date with his roommate and girlfriend. While we were all chatting in the dim light of the wine bar, I noticed that Andrew's phone kept lighting up with texts. The one that caught my eye had a heart-eyes emoji. I asked him who he was texting right now, on our date? He said it was just his gym coach, they were exchanging song recommendations. My palms started sweating. *Exchanging songs and heart emojis? Doesn't sound the most platonic to me.* For the first time in our whole relationship, my trust faltered.

And the grand finale: we went on a rowdy cabin trip for the Fourth of July with all of my friends. Having just received the not-ready-to-move-in news, plus the awful news about my grandma, I was not doing well. I hid it all behind a happy face as best I could, until I got one too many drinks in me. Eventually, the dam broke and I started sobbing. Only a few of my friends knew what was going on, and I was normally a cheerful drunk, so I have to imagine my tearful breakdown was disconcerting for everyone around me, including and especially Andrew. The rest of the weekend was awkward and upsetting, as Andrew clearly didn't want to be there and I felt a sickening mixture of embarrassment and fore-boding grief.

A couple of days after coming home, Andrew called and told me he needed some space to think things over. *Oh god, space. No, no, no!* My worst nightmare was coming true. The man I loved—my person, my whole future—was pulling away from me. I asked him how much space and he said a few days. I agreed reluctantly and let the phone fall from my ear as we hung up. My hand was weak and shaky with despair as I gripped my phone, willing him to call back. I stared at his name in the call log with the purple heart next to it. I gingerly tapped into his contact and hesitated for a moment before deleting the heart.

A few days later, he was at my door handing me a small box of my things. It took a moment for me to take the box; I didn't want to hold it because it meant the ending was real.

"Don't you think we can just work on things?" I pleaded as I grabbed lightly onto his wrist.

"No, I just can't," he answered softly. "I don't know why, but I can't. I just...I...don't love you enough."

Tears streamed torrentially down my cheeks. I tried to wipe them with the heels of my hands, but the saline sadness poured relentlessly down my wrists. There was no hiding from this. There was no pulling him back close to me again.

My arms fell limply by my sides as he walked out of my door for the last time, severing the future I'd already been living in. Teaching me, in a single, wretched moment, the danger of building homes in other people.

CHAPTER TEN

The 23-Year-Old

Have you ever been scared of an entire day of the week? I have.

Before I knew what "Sunday Scaries" meant colloquially, I thought maybe, possibly, other people felt the crushing weight of the altogether-too-much free time my Sundays in 2016 had become. After Andrew and I broke up and my grandma died within the same month, Sunday always scraped by, threatening to rip into my barely-together exterior with all of its jagged teeth. By jagged teeth, I mean the spare minutes and hours that contained all of the grief I didn't know how to feel. The homes I knew—the one inside Andrew, the one where my grandma could fix anything with a back scratch and buttered wheat toast, the one where my mom was impervious rather than listless and heartbroken—were gone forever. I longed to go back to the place where everyone I ever loved would come back to me, whole. That is to say, I longed for a home that didn't exist.

Have you ever been terrified of a city street? A neighborhood? An entire city? I have.

I couldn't go anywhere near where I might see Andrew, or be reminded of him, or see anyone or anything connected to him whatsoever. The whole city was suddenly a graveyard of all of my severed love that had nowhere to go. My life felt like a horror movie except all of the horrors were ordinary things. Whole Foods. The train station where we used to commute together. Pierce Street. Sweet potatoes. 4 p.m. The Lululemon store. The day after my birthday. The time between being with friends. The 27th of the month, when yet another whole month had almost passed and I wasn't over him. Being at home. Being anywhere. Being.

♡ ♡ ♡

That was the state I was in when I forced myself, in a silent "fuck you" to Andrew, to join a CrossFit gym (he'd always wanted me to do it when we were together). Within a few days of joining, I realized how much I loved it. It became the outlet for *all* of my energy and attention. Newly single people often get a dog or a haircut or a new wardrobe...but not me. I became a crossfitter. This is where I met the 23-year-old.

He was a gregarious, tall, broad-shouldered blonde who I almost didn't notice at first (because for some reason my hot-man-scanning radar is tuned almost exclusively to brunettes). I was 27 and the age difference felt like a Big Deal but as the weeks went by, I started looking for excuses to talk to him. He'd offer me friendly advice on my weightlifting form and I'd stare in awe as he threw an insanely heavy barbell into the air with ease.

Much to my delight, he started flirting with me and eventually asked me out to dinner and a concert. I accepted with glee. Suddenly the mountain of grief that I was hiding inside didn't feel so consuming. I was about three months out from my breakup with Andrew and (subconsciously) looking for someone new to build a home in. *Maybe I'm actually getting over it! I've already found someone new and so much better!* (There I was, trying to skip my grief again. It didn't work this time either.)

The concert went even better than I expected. He took my hand and led me through the crowd as we sang along to the bouncy music. We danced and smiled and kissed late into the night. I tucked that euphoric memory into a cozy nook of my brain; the one that held all of my happy memories. The only place inside of me I would visit on purpose, to replay my favorite moments and sink into a comfortable, hopeful languor. Inside this cozy nook, a new fantasy future was forming and I did nothing to slow it down. I started to fall hard for the 23-year-old as we went on more dates. We went beer-tasting together, spent Halloween together, and even commuted to work together sometimes on the train—him to his hip tech startup and me to my safe but slightly boring engineering job. He started inviting me to stay over and I was so enamored with him that I told myself I didn't even care that his room consisted of a mattress on the floor and several scattered piles of detritus. (Another funny dichotomy of SF tech guys: making six figures but living like they don't believe in furniture.)

During our sleepovers, he eventually started trying to hook up with me. I was on board in theory, but my body had other plans. Every time we'd intensely make out and it was starting to lead to more, my body would get extremely hot and red. It was so extreme that even he noticed and would ask if I was okay. I always told him I was fine, and I thought I was, but it was, one might say, quite the cock-block. (I learned years later when it happened again that this was my body telling me I was nowhere near comfortable enough or emotionally ready to have sex.)

Despite my overheating issue, we continued to deepen our relationship (or so I thought). By the time the holidays rolled around, I felt things were going well enough that I invited him to be my date to my company holiday party. He said yes and I was ecstatic, both about the implied meaning of him coming, and because I'd never had a real date to an official, fancy company party before!

The party came and everything seemed to go perfectly. I wore a black lace dress and looked my hottest for him; he was the perfect date, dapper and friendly. Afterward, the next day, we headed up to the mountains together to go snowboarding. On the drive home, he dropped a very unexpected piece of news on me: he only wanted to be friends with me because he felt emotionally unavailable and had never had a successful relationship before. *WHAT?! Again? How did I pick ANOTHER emotionally unavailable person?!* I could do nothing except nod understandingly but inside I started to feel the sullen, inky darkness spreading. I was not okay. I had never been okay. He was just a distraction from all of my not-okayness. As we drove into the sunset, I braced myself for the tidal wave of everything inside of me I had been avoiding.

I Had a Good Childhood, Why Is Love So Hard for Me?

This question used to keep me up at night, rattling around relentlessly inside my head. I felt like a fraud hiding a shameful secret. I had loving parents and an ostensibly idyllic childhood. Nothing majorly traumatic happened to me that I could recall. And yet, I constantly found myself struggling deeply with romantic relationships, seemingly much more so than my friends.

I still vividly remember the bottomless void of depression and loneliness I felt after my first major heartbreak. I was 19 and he, a year younger than me, had just left for college. He decided he wanted to be single for this new chapter, and I felt the most overwhelming hopelessness I'd ever felt in my life. I was listless. An empty shell of myself. Life had lost its color. My parents and friends tried their best to support me, but my depression was incorrigible. I could barely eat. For a while, this fit inside the realm of normal heartbreak. I received all of the compassion you'd expect after ending a multi-year first-love relationship. Yet my grieving process seemed to go on endlessly.

"Lauren, you've got to move on," my best friend would tell me lovingly, after I would cry to her about the same feelings for months on end. And eventually, I did "move on," but only by getting into another relationship. And then another. Yet each breakup would feel almost equally devastating. It would take me years to feel like I was truly over the person. I was haunted by my pain, and that constant, shame-ridden question: I had a good childhood, why am I SO messed up? I knew other people had it much worse, and they seemed okay, so what was wrong with me?

My shame was worsened by a lot of the standard breakup advice:

The best way to get over someone is by getting under someone else.

It takes half the amount of time you dated someone to get over them.

Distract yourself so that you don't have time to feel sad.

Needless to say, none of those "strategies" worked for me. The thought of "getting under someone else" after a breakup made me want to throw up. I was always sad well past the "recommended" grief deadline. Distracting myself felt like trying to put a band-aid on a broken bone.

I started to piece together how uncomfortable or unpracticed most people are with grief. We're often pressured by our emotionally constipated society to stuff or bypass our difficult emotions. Grief and despair are not openly discussed. Loss and death are often swept under the rug in place of easier-to-digest, copacetic platitudes.

After a soul-shattering breakup with someone I thought I'd marry and a subsequent unsuccessful rebound attempt, I realized that I couldn't keep living out this pattern. I stopped dating and started to delve into what was causing me to feel so egregiously not okay when I was alone. I started going to therapy (sometimes twice per week) and meditating every day. I was really hoping for a silver bullet and a quick-fix; perhaps something that would reveal itself during therapy, or some forgotten memory that my subconscious would spit up during meditation.

But I never found it.

Instead, I learned, with patient persistence, that it doesn't always take a Trauma with a capital T to inflict damage on your sensitive young self's psyche. It was okay—normal even—to feel a slew of difficult emotions without an obvious Traumatic Event in childhood. When I read the quote below from Gabor Mate, a trauma expert, it felt like a breath of fresh air. A validation of the struggle I had questioned for years:

"Trauma is not restricted to horrific experiences. It refers to any set of events that, over time, impose more pain on the child than his or her sensitive organism can process and discharge. Therefore, trauma can occur not only when bad things happen, but also when the parents are too stressed, too distracted, too depressed, too beset by economic worry, too isolated, etc. to respond to a sensitive child's emotional need to be seen, emotionally held, heard, validated, made to feel secure. Such is the reality behind many a story of 'happy childhood.'"

This understanding was monumental in allowing me to access a lot of difficult emotions that I had pushed down with the flawed belief that I shouldn't be so upset over "nothing." For me, that "nothing" turned out to be my beloved nanny skipping town and never returning when I was two years old, compounded by having an alcoholic parent who didn't get sober until later in my child-hood. These issues had always seemed like nothing to me, because

I didn't meaningfully remember any of the effects and because they seemed like small fish compared to other people's "real problems." But when I realized how these same pains of abandonment, loneliness, and being forgotten about replayed constantly in all of my romantic relationships, I understood how deeply I'd been affected. I came to accept how hurt and confused Little Me must have been while living through this.

With the help of somatically-focused meditation methods like body scans and breathwork, I began to understand how there was a lot more to healing than just intellectualizing the past. The first time I sat down to do a body-scan meditation (where you slowly and intentionally notice all parts of your body, one by one, starting from your head, down to your toes), I got to the top of my chest and felt a big knot of emotion bubble up to my throat. I let it arise and cried the deepest cry I'd had in a long, long time. It was somehow about both nothing and everything. There was all of this emotion stored inside my body that couldn't be unearthed by any amount of "thinking." Once I divorced from my over-functioning intellect, I finally gave my body the space it needed to feel.

♡ ♡ ♡

Your trauma is probably much different than mine. Maybe you had a Trauma with a capital T, and maybe you didn't. Maybe your trauma happened a long time ago, or maybe more recently. Maybe your trauma is from your family or maybe it's from a soul-shattering breakup or other loss. But trying to assign a magnitude to your own trauma in order to determine how deeply, or for how long you should be allowed to feel upset, is inherently *flawed. We are all entitled to our emotional experiences, regardless of what caused them. Emotions aren't up for debate, they just are. The truth is, you may never make logical sense of why you are the way you are. Your emotions may never fit inside a schedule, a box, or an explanation. But what if you can still accept yourself anyway?*

The best decision I ever made for my emotional health was to just accept where I was. To accept that yes, I still feel twinges of grief over that breakup years ago. Yes, I still burst into tears when I read old notes from my late grandma. Yes, I still occasionally miss my yellow Lab that died ages ago. Yes, I've cried over minor rejections. Yes, I feel the crushing weight of loneliness at times and on Sunday afternoons in particular. I stopped judging my emotions or trying to shoo them away for being of inappropriate magnitude.

Instead, I started listening and getting curious about what my emotions were inviting me to heal. What I kept finding was a wounded child, begging to not be cast aside. To be listened to and validated. To be told that it's okay to feel what she feels, for as long as she feels it. Once I gave myself permission to just feel how I already felt, I noticed that the despair and darkness started to pass through me, rather than staying stuck. I realized that the welcoming of all parts of yourself is what true freedom tastes like.

Finally, I was able to answer that relentless question: love was hard for me because I had been at war with myself. I had been unknowingly denying my own emotional experiences and thereby shutting off my heart to real, vulnerable connection. I had not been fully letting in the dark, the tumult, the grief that needed desperately to be felt so that it could be released. Love had been hard for me because I'd been treating it like a one-way street. The way in was wide open and meticulously swept, but the way out was blocked with the thorny overgrowth of unprocessed emotion.

As I invited all those shunned parts of me to have a seat at the table, to have a voice, to tell me what they had to say after all this time, I began to understand that love wasn't this unattainable thing outside of me. Love had been there the whole time, underneath it all; a tenacious flame flickering deep within my center. The only difference was, now I could access it. The feeling was unmistakable, like light leaking from my eyes and flowers spilling from my mouth and honey bleeding from my skin. Love always had been mine for the feeling.

PART THREE

Dark Night of the Soul

(27–30 years old)

Qualifications for dating me: in touch with his emotions, creative, not toxically masculine, has been to therapy or at least talks about wanting to go to therapy

CHAPTER ELEVEN
The Low-Key Soulmate—Part II

There are few feelings worse than having to turn around
from your own haughty saunter into the sunset and face the
ends you left carelessly untied. Once the blinding luster of
the fantasy with Andrew was extinguished, I came crawling
back to my regular life carrying a sickening realization of
how poorly I'd treated Miles a year prior. Ironically it was
only after experiencing someone I deeply loved pull away
from me suddenly that I understood the unique and searing
pain I'd caused Miles. I had never felt more sorry in my life.
Even if he was only feeling a fraction of the pain I felt, I absolutely hated myself for causing it.

So, a while after my breakup with Andrew, I reached out
to Miles with a text that was apologetic and unassuming. I
had no idea if he'd ever want to talk to me again, and rightfully so. I wanted so badly to apologize to him in person for
how I'd treated him and to explain how much I'd learned
since we last talked. Much to my surprise, he replied with
equanimity and, after a few texts, agreed to meet up with me
to have a conversation.

We met up the following week at our favorite Caribbean restaurant and any tension that had built up during our time apart quickly melted away. I felt instantly at ease in his presence and I could tell from the glint in his eye, behind the remaining hurt, that he was really happy to see me too. He had just gotten out of a relationship too and we bonded over our shared experiences of dating someone who was good on paper but just wasn't "it." (At this point I was somewhere between the "anger" and "bargaining" stages of grieving Andrew, so realistically I was resentfully fantasizing about him realizing his big mistake and coming back to me. But for sanity purposes, I only allowed myself to talk out loud about how we obviously weren't right for each other.)

Eventually, we got to talking about our dissolution and Miles explained more details about the night at the club and the weeks surrounding it. Up until that point, I thought I'd hidden everything pretty well, but Miles had picked up on me dating Andrew and was only further hurt by my secrecy. I apologized profusely for everything. I had a rudimentary understanding of my penchant for chasing unavailable men at that time, so I explained how that played into my decisions, and how I was completely blind to Miles's kindness and availability. He graciously accepted my apology and the wall between us crumbled down.

We began to gravitate toward each other again, inevitably and without regard. Since we were both newly single and I had the emotional capacity of a piece of toast at the time, it felt relatively safe to be close to him again. (Plus he was unendingly kind in helping me heal from Andrew, especially when I found out the vomit-inducing news that Andrew *was* dating his CrossFit coach shortly after we broke up.) Miles and I acknowledged that we were each way too broken for anything "real" so our friendship soon morphed into a "friends with benefits" arrangement. Neither of us had any experience in this kind of relationship but we figured hey, what's the worst that can happen? We made a pact to discontinue if and when either of us caught feelings. And that was that.

For months, our arrangement worked splendidly. Once again I felt myself questioning conventional wisdom, this time about the difficulty of maintaining a "friend with benefits." *Pshh! Who says you can't casually sleep with your friend? It's easy and fun as long as you just openly communicate!* Seemingly, neither Miles nor I were catching feelings, but we were having the best time together! We took more road trips, I met his parents and grandparents as his "friend," and we even traveled to Colombia together—a country we'd both dreamed of visiting.

A while after that trip, he sheepishly admitted that he was starting to develop feelings for me again. I was still too heartbroken to have real feelings for anyone, but I respected him for telling me and we agreed to slow down on our "arrangement." In practice, this meant that we'd hang out a little bit less, stop sleeping together, and each attempt to date other people. Those "other people" were all comically wrong for me, and I'd usually find myself on dates wishing I was hanging out with Miles instead. This was the first clue I had feelings for him, but I completely missed it because I didn't feel that addictive pull toward him—the one that comes from wanting someone you can't have. Instead I felt comfort and ease, which, sadly, were not feelings I associated with love, then.

Despite our agreement to slow down, Miles and I kept spending large swaths of time together. It was during one of these swaths, when Miles took me backpacking for the first time, that I realized I had feelings for him too. We were driving back from Yosemite and in my tired stupor, I left my wallet in a Chipotle but didn't realize it until we were almost home. Chipotle couldn't mail it to me for security reasons, so our only option was to drive back. I mapped it out and it was a three-hour round-trip. I usually despise driving but to my surprise, I didn't mind the thought of three more hours in the car with Miles at *all*. *If I have to spend three hours with anyone right now, I'm so happy it's him!* In that moment, I knew something had irreversibly shifted inside of me.

Uh-oh.

I didn't tell Miles about my revelation. I didn't quite understand the feelings myself; my emotional interior still felt like a messy, unintelligible tangle. All I could obviously feel was the still-loud grief over Andrew. So instead, I pushed my nebulous maybe-love for Miles aside, certain it'd pass. Some (likely avoidant) part of me convinced me that we weren't right for each other anyway. We'd never work; he was too nice and I'd walk all over him. He liked me too much, it made me feel uncomfortable and too…seen.

Thus began another era of push-pull, but this time I was on the other side.

♡ ♡ ♡

A month or so after the Chipotle wallet incident, Miles took me to my very first Burning Man. It took some serious convincing—I hated the heat and I didn't consider myself the "Burner type"—but he assured me I would love it. He had been a few times, so he was seasoned and helped me prepare for a week in the grueling heat and dust. Apparently, my festival expertise from Coachella and the like would *in no way* prepare me for Burning Man, according to anyone who had ever gone (which seemed to be at least half of San Francisco).

As soon as we arrived and biked out to the surreal, art-filled expanse at sunset, I was so grateful to Miles for convincing me to come. I watched a world unfold in front of me that I thought could only exist in dreams: a huge orange dragon on wheels bumped across the desert, crossing paths with an oversized floating cupcake. A retro speed boat drove past with tons of people dancing onboard. It glittered with a teal and pink aesthetic, as if it had somehow just arrived from an 80s Miami. People were climbing up a skewered stack of vintage cars (yes, like a car-kebab) in the distance and swinging on a 50-foot-tall swing set in the foreground, the top of which seemed to be disappearing into the clouds. Next to me, people scaled five levels of scaffolding to wait their turn to zipline. I accepted a nearby stranger's megaphone invitation to try their camp's giant slide. There was no catch or complication, it was just play for play's sake. I flew down the slide with a wild smile, quietly heartened by how well Miles *knew* me. I *did* love it there. I had never seen a more magical place in my life.

A few days into the week, as we sat on plush floor pillows at 4 a.m. recovering from the night out, he asked me a question that had been clattering around in my own mind too:

"Do you ever wonder if we're, like, low-key soulmates?"

"I wonder that all the time," I told him, because our connection felt undeniable despite not even being in a real "relationship."

"I think I love you more than anyone I've ever loved," he then admitted, almost matter-of-factly. It was unlike him to be this vulnerable with me given our "status" of late, so I knew he must still be a little bit drunk. I was too, so I didn't fully feel the weight of his words until later. As the week progressed, his question burrowed into my chest and my maybe-we're-soulmates feelings for him started to claw their way out of the cage I'd locked them in. I kept trying to find ways to be alone with him, which was exceedingly difficult because we were camped with a bunch of friends.

Finally, on the second-to-last night, we broke away from everyone to go admire the bright, mysterious art installations nearby. As we neared a giant sign that glowed blueish-green, we slowed and hopped off our bikes. *This is my chance!* I turned to Miles, smiled, and playfully threw him to the ground to kiss him. He kissed me back and as we separated, laughing, I was taken aback by the cinematic beauty of the moment. His eyes reflected the neon light from the sign behind us that read, "Everything you need is inside you." *Is it though?* Everything I wanted was inside of him.

♡ ♡ ♡

After Burning Man, Miles and I continued to try and distance ourselves but the movies of us played in my head relentlessly, like a shitty 24-hour movie marathon I couldn't mute. I came *so* close to blurting out that I loved him during that magical moment at the neon sign. It was all I could think about. *What if?* I was fantasizing at full tilt and the more he seemingly pulled away from me, the more I obsessed. He even vaguely mentioned he was seeing someone new, but I brushed it aside as an easily-surmountable hurdle. How could he ask if we were soulmates, but date someone else? No, no, I'd work for his love and convince him to be with me. There it was: the addictive pull. He was becoming someone I couldn't have— someone whose love I had to work for—and *nothing* could have drawn me to him more.

One November morning, after we hadn't talked for a few weeks, I woke up and *still* couldn't get him off my mind. So I made a compromise with myself: I'd write him a letter. I'd corral all of this emotion by putting words around it and I'd give him the letter at an undetermined "later" time (months later, I figured). I spent three hours in a Philz coffee shop ferociously penning all of my overflowing love (or what I thought was love) onto paper. I told him he was the only person in the world who made me feel safe. I told him that when I tabulated all of my favorite recent memories, he was in every single one. I told him that I was sorry for being so emotionally closed off and for breaking his heart. I told him that it took me years, but I was finally able to accept a love like his. I told him that I loved him. (I whole-heartedly believed I was in love with him then, but was I actually in love with *him*? Not quite. I was mostly in love with the idealized version of him in my head. *Sigh.*)

After leaving the coffee shop and wandering around aimlessly for a bit, I begrudgingly convinced myself to get groceries. It was Sunday and I loathed too-crowded Sunday evening grocery shopping but I needed to think about *anything* other than Miles. As I walked into Trader Joe's, there was Miles, right in front of the broccoli. *Are you serious right now, Universe?*

"Oh, hey stranger!" I chirped, feigning coyness as my entire body vibrated with emotion. We then shopped together and laughed about the silly things our families did over Thanksgiving. It felt the same, but different; he seemed distant in a way I couldn't put my finger on. After we checked out, he waited for me outside and we chatted more, both lingering a bit. Neither of us *really* wanted to leave, but we kept it short and hugged goodbye. I knew I couldn't wait a moment longer to give him my letter.

Later that night, I biked the four blocks to his house and handed him the folded pages. I told him to read it and let me know when he wanted to talk. He texted me an hour later: **Your letter made me cry. I don't know what to do. I respect your words so much, but I have to tell you that I'm dating someone.** My heart fell into the padded state of disappointment I'd prepared for this response. *Ugh! It figures. But still, fuck!* He came over later that night, teary-eyed, and we had a "closure" conversation; he admitted that he shared some feelings for me too but remained firm on his decision to stay with his new girlfriend. My worst nightmare was coming true: Unrequited Love.

"I'm not going to forget about you. I know you worry about that. But don't," he assured me sweetly. He said that if he and I were ever going to be together in the future, we needed to choose each other, and right now he couldn't choose me. *Only right now?* I memorized that sliver of hope and tossed it into my ever-growing fantasy collection, which I'd later use to cope instead of accepting Miles had moved on. I felt inexplicably suffocated when he left my house that night because I didn't know how to exist on my own without the slow drip of validation from a guy. For three years, Miles had been there as a sort of subconscious backup plan and now that he was gone, I was left alone with someone I felt uncomfortable with and didn't know very well: myself.

CHAPTER TWELVE

The Twice–My–Age Reddit Penpal

I've always been an early-adopter type with everything internet-related; I was downloading mp3s on Napster and building an empire on Neopets as soon as I learned how to use the World Wide Web. So naturally, it follows that in my early 20s, I stumbled across Reddit, otherwise known as "the front page of the internet." At first I mostly "lurked," meaning I just read content and didn't post. But soon I started using it to crowd-source arguments between Nico and me back when we were dating, or more embarrassingly, to validate my attractiveness level.

It was during one such validation attempt that I encountered Keith. I'd been having bad luck in dating, so I decided to post to the subreddit "Am I Ugly?" just to make sure I wasn't missing out on some glaring issue with my face or body. (The internet is *always* the best place to go for feedback on your appearance, right?) I posted a few pictures and was summarily told I wasn't ugly. *Phew!!!* One of the commenters, who I'd later come to know as Keith, gave me some kind reassurance: *It's definitely not your looks; perhaps you're having trouble because of your insecurity?* He was definitely right about that, but I didn't understand it then, nor would I understand it for the next half-decade.

Keith and I then started exchanging private Reddit messages and getting to know each other. We had a surprising amount in common despite him living in Tennessee with his wife and me living my mostly-single life in California. He was also 46 years old to my 23, but we quickly found common ground with how our brains worked; we were both engineers who thrived within the realms of logic and intellect. We took turns giving each other advice and feedback on the various goings-on of our lives; he helped guide me through some dating issues, and I helped explain certain interpersonal struggles he was having. He remained relatively tight-lipped about his marriage, but every now and then I'd offer feedback there too (only when asked, of course).

Months passed, and then years. We remained connected casually via Reddit messages. A couple of years in, he let me know that he was struggling in his marriage. I offered my condolences and a listening ear if he needed it. He didn't provide many details and I didn't pry.

Another year passed and we decided to try and meet up. We both had upcoming vacations to Europe and would be in Munich at the same time for Oktoberfest. Before this trip, he hadn't mentioned me much to his wife but since they'd be traveling together, he made sure that meeting up with a random girl half his age from the internet was okay with her. She was fine with it, he said, and we set a time and place to meet.

Our plans to meet went awry when my phone battery bugged out in Europe and stopped holding a charge. On the day we were supposed to meet, my friends refused to let me go off alone with an almost-dead phone, to meet an older man from Reddit (they were right). Just before my phone completely died, I sent Keith a couple of texts explaining the situation and telling him which beer tent I was in, hoping he'd come find me. He never came. It turned out, his phone wasn't set up to receive texts while in Europe, so he ended up waiting with his wife at our supposed meeting spot for a long time. This only angered his already-annoyed wife more. Once I got back to my Airbnb the next morning (yes, morning...the dead-phone situation caused me to get lost in Munich for 12 hours, but I digress), I tried to explain to Keith what happened but the damage had been done. He'd apparently done a lot of convincing to get his wife to agree to meet me, and then I'd left them waiting. Keith was very angry and told me that I was inconsiderate and he was done talking to me. We didn't talk for a year and a half.

♡ ♡ ♡

By 2016, the tension had calmed and Keith and I began exchanging messages again. Lightly. He'd reached out and, after some explanation, he forgave me for the Munich debacle and apologized for getting so upset. Soon after we began talking again, my life imploded with the Andrew breakup and my grandma's death. I decided that what I needed was a solo trip, to like, find myself or whatever. I'd never been to

Nashville and it sounded trendy and fun, so I booked flights and a hostel stay. Nashville also happened to be a few-hour drive from Keith, so I decided to combine my trip with a visit to him and his wife. (I should mention that I had video chatted with Keith many times over the years, so it wasn't like I was blindly visiting a complete stranger from the internet. But still, very questionable decision-making, I know.) He invited me to stay over in their extra bedroom for a couple of nights and assured me that he and his wife were on good terms now and she was 100% good with me coming to visit. *Great! I can finally meet them both!*

Upon arriving, the minimal worry I did have about meeting a much older internet man and his wife disappeared. They were both welcoming and sweet, immediately offering to cook me a homemade dinner. We then had margaritas on the couch and fell into comfortable and engaging conversation. Keith's wife was easy to talk to and it seemed she liked me too.

Whether it was naivete or stupidity, the thought of anything romantic between Keith and me never, *ever* crossed my mind. Him being twice my age (and married!) was enough to make our relationship obviously and forever platonic, to me. Needless to say, I was *extremely* surprised when, on the second day of my visit, after he and I had gone on a hike, he pulled his truck over to a vista point and politely asked if he could kiss me. *Uhhhhh.* I was at a loss for words. He explained that he'd assumed my intentions in coming to visit may have had more-than-platonic undertones, so he asked for a hall pass from his wife to kiss me and she'd agreed. *What?!* That made me feel even weirder. I stumbled over my words as I tried to tactfully explain that I had no intention or interest in kissing him.

He accepted my rejection graciously and we continued on, mostly pretending it didn't happen. When we got home, we had an early dinner together with his wife, who had been on her own hike with a different friend. Armed with this new, very strange "hall pass" information, I put on my less-naive goggles and tried to detect any weirdness from her or Keith. I couldn't sense anything. She seemed just as friendly as before, and he didn't seem put off by me. *Well, this is awkward as fuck for ME, but I guess it's...fine?* I was certainly not going to be the one to mention the attempted kiss, and everything seemed okay enough, so I tried to just brush the whole thing aside.

The next morning, I decided to leave Keith's a bit early so I could have more time in Nashville. I told him (privately) that it had nothing to do with the kiss thing—despite it definitely having something to do with the kiss thing—and we left everything on good terms. As I pulled out of the driveway waving goodbye to Keith and his wife, I concluded that the visit went quite well. The kiss attempt was just a small blemish on an otherwise lovely couple of days.

A few days later, after thanking Keith for my visit, I received a series of messages from him explaining how he could no longer be in contact with me because I was so "draining" to him, among other reasons. He danced around a "specific phrase" that he didn't want to say directly but strongly implied something like narcissistic personality disorder. He said that his wife saw it too, and she was, in fact, the one who suggested that he Google this "specific phrase." He requested that I do not reply to his message. He then sent one last email with a post-it note quote about selfishness and signed the email #mourningthelossofafriend.

I was *floored*. I had no idea how he (or his wife) gathered any of this from my visit. As far as I remembered, I was polite and thankful. I expressed appreciation multiple times for dinner, drinks, and anything else that was offered to me. I racked my brain for *any* evidence of egregious disregard on my part that would lead to Keith's conclusion. I couldn't think of a single thing. I came to the only conclusion that made sense to me: Keith was bitter over the kiss rejection and decided to chew me out. I was pissed. I sent him a scathing reply a few days later and assumed I'd never talk to him again.

♡ ♡ ♡

Many more years later, Keith waved a white flag and reached out. He let me know that he may have misjudged me all those years ago and that he and his wife were on the verge of divorce. I was still wary of him, so I kept my distance, but I was dying for an explanation from the aftermath of my visit. A few months after his reach-out, he let me know that his wife left him in the middle of the night. Some combination of raw curiosity, forgiveness, and questionable judgment caused me to start talking to him again. He immediately explained that after my visit, his wife completely demonized me and made him cut me off. *Guess she wasn't cool with my visit, or a kiss, or anything after all, huh?* After having matured a few years, I kind of took her side. *Yeah, Keith, your wife probably wasn't a huge fan of you fraternizing with a much younger woman. Why would she be?* He understood, took full responsibility, and we began to build a friendship again—this time strictly platonic on *both* sides.

I had unintentionally learned my second (but not last) painful lesson about interacting with married men: marriage does not always stop a man from trying to make a move. Also, after my now *two* disastrous experiences, I would forever steer clear of anything to do with hall passes.

CHAPTER THIRTEEN
The Maybe–Love–Addict (Me)

After the aforementioned events of my late 20s that could only be described as a dumpster fire, I knew something (or many things) had to change. My questionable judgment and crippling insecurity seemed to continually get me into frustrating situations. It felt like I wasn't actually healing, but instead, continuously un-attaching my pain from one man and attaching it to another.

I was already in traditional talk therapy but I decided I needed more. I started to look into every therapy or healing modality that I could find. I tried Reiki. I tried a psychic. I tried past-life readings. I tried yoga. I tried EMDR. I tried different styles of meditation, including holotropic breathwork (a.k.a purposeful hyperventilating that can make you hallucinate!). I tried new-age methods that you've never even heard of. I eventually even started attending 12-step meetings for sex and love addicts. I needed an explanation for how I felt. I *needed* to understand why I was struggling so much. Why, after a year—despite *knowing* we weren't right for each other—I wasn't over Andrew. Why my grieving process felt never-ending and why I felt so pathetic about it. Why I acted avoidant and pushed Miles away and only became obsessed with him once he was no longer available. Why I felt so unattractive and unworthy. Why I felt like I might *actually* be alone forever.

♡ ♡ ♡

"Hi. I'm Lauren, I'm a love addict."

I repeated this phrase weekly in Sex and Love Addicts Anonymous (SLAA) meetings, but the words always felt blocky and foreign inside my mouth. Was I a love addict? I honestly wasn't sure. When we'd read the Characteristics of Sex and Love Addiction every meeting, I'd find myself resonating with at least half of them. *Feeling empty and incomplete when alone?* Yup. *Becoming immobilized or seriously distracted by romantic obsessions or fantasies.* Definitely. *Assigning magical qualities to others, idealizing and pursuing them, then blaming them for not fulfilling our fantasies and expectations?* Ugh, dammit, yes.

But then I'd listen to the three-minute allotted shares of the other people in the meetings, and I'd feel like an alien, like I didn't really belong there at all. I wasn't upending my whole life for love or sex. I wasn't really "acting out," meaning I wasn't texting my exes, or outwardly pursuing men who were obviously bad for me, or having unsafe sex with random people from bars. My issues were mostly internal: my coping strategies consisted of ruminating over the past or fantasizing about my various exes coming back rather than dealing with the grief and pain of (perceived) abandonment. This somehow felt *more* impossible to fix because it was just *how my brain worked* (or so I thought, then).

Regardless, I wanted to give the program a fair try. I had some family members who had major success with AA, so I had faith in the 12-step process. In one of my first few meetings, I found a sponsor—a strikingly beautiful woman in her 30s whose stories I related to, and whose growth I was in awe of. In my eyes, she could probably have any guy she wanted, but instead she was prioritizing her healing. I desperately wanted to feel that composed, that unconcerned. I desperately wanted to feel that un-desperate.

Under her guidance, I started the 12-step process. The first step was admitting I was powerless over my love addiction. I considered the events of my recent past—pining over Miles, fantasizing about him constantly, fantasizing over Andrew coming back—and I tried on "feeling powerless" over all of this. I guess that was a fair term for it. I acquiesced (to my journal and my sponsor) and moved on to steps 2 and 3: believing in a power higher than myself that could restore my sanity, and turning my will over to that higher power. This brushed up against my distaste for "God" in a religious sense, but I took a more spiritual approach and used a more diffuse higher power, something like nature or the Universe. Next was taking a moral inventory of myself—of my wrongs and character defects. I walked through all my relationships and journaled about my flaws and mistakes: the selfishness, the "hall pass" with Nico, the avoidance, the validation-seeking from other men when I was in a relationship, the

burdening of my friends and family with my constant rumination, the carelessness with Miles's feelings. I began to look
for the ways I was participating in these romantic fiascos I
kept getting into, rather than just blaming the men.

As I worked the steps, my desire to heal was always at
odds with my crippling fear of being alone. My sponsor *heav-
ily* suggested I take 90 days "sober" and don't date at all. This
was hard for me to commit to. The more time I spent single
and not doing anything tangible about it, the more terror
would take root in my bones, rattling me with some version
of this same question: *What if you are too old, all the good ones
are gone, and you end up alone?* So, once I felt somewhat emotionally stable—assisted by the training wheels of all the
therapy modalities I had endeavored in—I did what I figured
I had to do. I took a deep, all-the-way-into-my-belly breath
and...downloaded the dating apps again. I didn't tell my
sponsor about this.

By then it was 2018, and the apps were catching on like
wildfire—everyone seemed to be on them. I had a few friends
who had recently met their partners on an app, which gave
me hope. I was looking for something serious, as I always
had been, but now it seemed like finding that was realistic,
rather than some edge-case luck story. I figured between
Hinge, Bumble, Tinder, Coffee Meets Bagel[10], The League,
and of course the old, reliable OKCupid, I was sure to find
one compatible match. I was more determined than ever.

---

10   Coffee Meets Bagel is one of the lesser known dating apps that claims 91%
     of its users are looking for a serious relationship.

Unfortunately, unbeknownst to me at the time, my determination was adulterated with hints of desperation, confusion, and a still-shaky sense of self. Thus began an experimental era of dating a lot of men who were, in short, humorously wrong for me.

CHAPTER FOURTEEN

The Whimsical Musician Who Wore Women's Bell Bottoms

If you've spent any time on dating apps, you know how they can go from *Wow! Exciting! So many options!* to *ALAS! I shall prepare for a life of celibacy and loneliness* pretty quickly. In other words, my relationship to the apps was tempestuous and inconsistent. On some days I'd have an abundance of matches and feel optimistically *certain* that I was just one date away from my soulmate. On other days, my forever-alone fear seemed to be coming to fruition, as the guys I was most excited about would stop replying. Or worse, they'd just wordlessly unmatch me and leave me to draw my own conclusions about why. On some days I'd feel self-assured and beautiful: *Of course these men are interested! I'm a catch!* On other days I felt despairing and apathetic: *The men I'm actually attracted to aren't interested in a woman like me; what the fuck is the point?*

These chaotic emotional fluctuations were making a mess of me, yet I felt beholden to the apps, because how else would

I ever meet someone? Meeting a guy in the wild felt like a dying dream of a bygone era, especially in San Francisco. I don't know how it is dating in other areas, but there's a famous saying about dating in Silicon Valley: The odds are good but the goods are odd. Meaning, due to the male-dominated tech industry, men do outnumber women, but because the date-ability of those men is often diminished by engineer-y awkwardness, Peter Pan syndrome, and career obsession, it is by no means "raining men" in these parts. Men in my day-to-day life would rarely make eye contact with me, let alone talk to me. At least the apps provided an easy way to ice-break romantic interest. So I kept swiping, messaging, swallowing my disappointment, changing my pictures, and tinkering with my profile until, finally, I'd find a decent match.

The first of these decent matches was Nathan. The mention of being sapiosexual on his Hinge profile piqued my interest and his not-tech career (creative advertising) sealed the deal. I needed a break from dating software engineers. I needed a man who was emotionally intelligent and didn't just apply logic to relationships. Nathan seemed like a promising new beginning, a reformation of "my type." So, I was extra pleased when he walked into the bar bespectacled, tall, and even cuter than his profile pictures.

Our first date consisted of flirting and only half paying attention during bar bingo. He *was* different from other guys I'd dated; he was a musician and lived a life centered around creativity. He seemed emotionally in tune, sensitive, and open-minded; a perfect combination of healthy traits according to what I'd learned in therapy and my 12-step group. We talked about what made dates fun and both agreed this was a top-tier first date. We won a polka-dot apron during bingo and he gave it to me, but not before making me take a photo in it atop my Vespa. He later sent me the photo and gushed that he had an amazing time. *A man who is just straightforward about his interest in me?* I felt that delicious sense of relief and hope that comes with validation of reciprocal interest after a great first date.

Our subsequent second date riding scooters to a scenic overlook was magical. We kissed on the hillside and bonded over our love of Manchego cheese. He played guitar for me and it was endearing and romantic. (Serenade update: I think it's the *singing* that makes serenades so awkward. Just guitar playing is very pleasant!)

Somewhere between the fourth and fifth date was when things started to go downhill. I started to realize he was a little *too* quirky for me. Like...making a sing-song out of everything, going to off-the-grid LSD weekend parties, painting his nails, squealing high-pitched giggles, and dressing like he's an ambassador for Burning Man kind of quirky. He fit right in with the hippie-Burner subculture that defined Haight-Ashbury. This was a foundational personality type of San Francisco that I hadn't tried dating prior to him, but alas, none of it (him) was working for me. Nothing about his mannerisms was inherently *wrong* (paint your nails and do psychedelics as you please), but I realized he was definitely wrong for *me*. Cue the dreaded "ick."

On our final date, we met at the park for a picnic and he was wearing very wide-leg bell bottoms and a sparkly jean vest. The ick intensified. I tried to look past it but felt my lady parts clamming up immediately. I was already feeling like I wasn't as attracted to him as I wanted to be, so this didn't help. Once we set up our hammock, he got to chatting with a guy sitting near us who was *also* wearing bell bottoms. The guy offered up a quick tip:

"You've got to buy them in the women's section; they have the best selection!"

Nathan agreed vehemently. And that was that. A budding romance swiftly crushed by a pair of second-hand women's pants.

CHAPTER FIFTEEN

The Overly Eager CEO Who Approached Me in Trader Joe's

I was standing in front of the hummus deliberating between eggplant and tomato basil when he walked up to me.

"Can I take a picture of your shirt? That's my friend's company!"

I was wearing a new shirt from a company in Austin. We got to chatting and he told me he had moved to San Francisco from Austin to start a company—a dating app! Was he a software engineer? I asked. No, he was the CEO. At the time I found this hot. We exchanged numbers and I walked out of the store with a major happy-bounce in my step. It felt refreshing to meet someone in person for once, and in Trader Joe's no less. Talk about a dream meet-cute story!

We started texting and he quickly asked me to hang out that same night. He said he wanted to cook for me. I already had dinner plans but he asked me to come over afterward. *Um, come over after dinner on a Wednesday? For a first date?* It was easy for me to say no because I now knew what this was a euphemism for, and I didn't put myself in situations to sleep with guys too early anymore. Regardless, his invitation should have been a warning sign about what he was looking for, but I was not about to let this picturesque in-the-wild meet-cute go that easily!

We made plans for brunch that weekend. He again insisted on wanting to cook for me so he invited me over for eggs and waffles. After breakfast he quickly made the move to his bedroom, claiming he was "too full" and needed to lie down. Again, this should have been a warning sign, but hey, it would at least be an interesting story right? A few minutes later while sitting on his bed, he dove into a story about his room-mate having a loud threesome, and then in the same breath grabbed me and started aggressively making out with me. I barely had time to process this bizarre sequence of events before noticing that, unfortunately for my general well-being, I did have quite a bit of physical chemistry with him. *This is how mistakes are made, isn't it?*

He continued this behavior throughout the rest of the date, showing excessive amounts of PDA as we walked to a park to hang out. Every time we stopped on a street corner, he'd grab me and make out with me. I felt incredibly uncomfortable but I didn't really know what to do. At the park, where we met up with some of my friends, he sat with his back to the conversation and opened his laptop to work. It was Sunday, but they had a code-commit deadline that evening, he said. How iconically tech-bro.

Later on, he asked me if I set my own work schedule and alluded to me coming over for a "midweek bang." At this point, I realized I had to slowly back away. We had one more date planned, which he stood me up for because he forgot to put it on his calendar. It appeared there were no real people or dating skills required to be the CEO of a dating app, which honestly explains a lot.

CHAPTER SIXTEEN

The Guy Who Was Leaving for Bali in Three Days

We met at one of those wine bars with a trendy two-word name containing food and some sort of wood: Fig & Birch, Olive & Thistle, Ham & Branch...something like that. Anyway, our chemistry was immediate and palpable. He sat on a stool next to me and leaned in, asking personal questions right away: *What's your ideal man like? Tell me more about your meditation practice? What is your attachment style?*

Fifteen minutes into the date, our knees were already touching. He ordered me another glass of Pinot Noir before I finished my first glass and then told me that he grew up with sisters, so he *really* understood women. He also told me he was leaving for Bali on Monday, three days from now, and mentioned how he couldn't wait to be off the grid.

"I don't really like having a cell phone. I just don't want to have to answer to anyone."

He was telling me that we probably weren't compatible, but I let it roll right off me. *Surely* he wasn't referring to people like me—women he had great chemistry with and kissed passionately on first dates. It was the best first date I'd had in ages. Maybe ever? It was so good that I wondered if he might be *it*. We had a second date the very next day. I went over to his house and we watched a show about outer space because I'd mentioned I love space facts. He asked me to stay over twice, which caught me a little off guard. He "knew women" but asked a woman who said she took things *very* slow to stay over on the second date? *Hmm*.

He left for Bali two days later. I never heard from him again. I spent the following month (okay, three months) in agonizing disbelief about the fact that we could have *such* an amazing first date and it ultimately meant nothing. It was those dates—the ones that inspired that rare, sparkly hope only to later turn to dust—that deteriorated my trust in myself. I blamed myself for reading the dates so wrong. For reading *him* so wrong. *Pathetic, Lauren, pathetic! How did you let this happen again? There must be something about you that repels men. Find it so this doesn't happen again!* I tirelessly combed through the details of our two dates, searching for evidence of where I was accidentally repulsive, clingy, or unattractive. I analyzed and re-analyzed everything he said, desperate to understand what clue I missed that would have tipped me off about his plan to never talk to me again. My search yielded nothing obvious, then. So I told myself I was an idiot for getting so excited and that I could never, under *any* circumstances, get that excited again. A corrosive jadedness began to take root inside me.

This experience, though a tiny blip in the grand scheme, represented my Achilles heel in dating: getting caught up in the fantasy of someone over the short-term instead of paying attention to who they *actually* were over time. I bought into short-term words instead of long-term actions because I didn't know any better. This, in essence, is what makes dating apps so challenging: they foster and even *encourage* short-term decision-making and snap judgments. You often only have one or two dates—maybe a few hours—to decide if someone is a romantic match for you. This potential match often comes with no context so all you have to go on is their word and early-date chemistry (and potentially their internet presence, if you digitally stalk them before a date). Chemistry is an excellent distraction from discernment and is often the counter-point to "taking things slow." To add more complication, some well-practiced daters are able to drum up chemistry with almost anyone, so it can be near-impossible to discern if someone is truly into you on those first couple dates, or if they're just good at dating.

This type of dating environment asks *a lot* of us daters, much of which we are never taught, but instead only learn with frustrating experience. We have to figure out how to withhold our trust for long enough to know if someone is trustworthy, but not so long that we're "guarded." We have to suppress our excitement after a great first date in the not-so-off chance that the person never texts us again, but not suppress it so much that we become jaded. We have to remember to take early-date chemistry with a grain of salt so that we can flirt back and have fun, but not get too attached (just in case). When we get ghosted, we have to practice "not taking it personally" with a Buddhist-monk level of composure, because despite knowing it's most certainly the ghoster's problem, it still feels like we somehow did something wrong. We have to pick ourselves back up and keep dating when, even after we thought we did e*verything* right last time, it still didn't work out. What a precarious and emotionally-taxing balance to maintain. No wonder burnout from app dating is so common!

The takeaway here is that it's *normal* and even *expected* to struggle with all of the snares and pitfalls of modern dating. It's impossible to get it right every time because people are unpredictable and emotions are messy. Yes, honing discernment, intuition, resilience, and patience in dating is extremely helpful (I certainly had lots of growth to be had in all of these areas), but even with all of these, app dating can bring you to your knees (not *that* way). It's *tough* out there. I wish someone had told me this when I was busy blaming myself for all of my dating "failures" and "misreads." We all deserve to give ourselves grace and remember that we weren't born experts at finding love on the internet.

CHAPTER SEVENTEEN

The Alarmingly Clingy
Starving Artist

We talked on the phone for a couple of hours before our first date. It was a refreshing change of pace to talk to a man who seemed so sensitive and emotionally in-tune (you may be sensing a theme). He was an artist and he painted a portrait of me before we met. A little strange in retrospect, but he was *so* different from other guys I'd dated and I was intrigued.

He brought me a Gerbera daisy—one of my favorite flowers—to our first date at a museum. It was a sweet gesture. Then he wanted to hold my hand immediately. *Um, sure?* We'd talked enough over the phone that I did feel moderately comfortable with him, but then we sat on a bench inside the museum and he wanted to put his arms around me. Not just one arm, like you normally would while sitting on a bench. Both arms. Wrapped around my torso. At this point, I started to get a little worried. Was he a Stage Five Clinger?

Yes. The answer was yes. The date just got weirder and weirder as he asked to record me with the Go-Pro he brought to the date. He said he made films and I was a great subject.

A powerful, beautiful woman. He kept filming me throughout the different exhibits and exclaiming how amazing I was. At this point, I felt pretty uncomfortable and ended the date as politely as I could.

As we walked back to BART (SF's underground metro) to go home, he asked to see me again. I told him I thought we weren't quite on the same page; it seemed like he felt really strongly about me and I couldn't match his feelings. He seemed to only half hear me because he texted me the next day asking for another date. I kindly turned him down. He replied with a paragraph text full of accusatory hostility, telling me I was "afraid of love." I ignored it.

Then the voicemails started. He kept calling, for days and days. I didn't block him because it was just too fascinating. He rambled on about how we'd "just had a misunderstanding" and should talk about it. He talked like we'd been dating for years and just needed to resolve our differences. After a few weeks, his calls eventually stopped and I realized I'd encountered the opposite extreme from being ghosted: someone being *way* too into me, and it was equally terrible. Why did the apps seem to only present me with caricatures and extremes? Where were the "just regularly into me" people?! They had to exist, right?

CHAPTER EIGHTEEN

The Low-Key Soulmate—Part III

A few months after my five-page love letter to Miles, I got a very surprising out-of-the-blue text from a mutual friend of ours:

Kinda weird question haha but do you still have feelings for Miles?[11]

My heart immediately started slamming against my chest as I replied sheepishly:

Haha yuuuup. It's been rough. Why do you ask?

She thought Miles and I should talk and that he might reach out soon. I could barely breathe. I felt like I'd just downed eight shots of espresso. I immediately called her and she explained that he'd been wrestling with his feelings for me and finally gave in to them. He was going to break up with his girlfriend, for me. *OH MY GOD.*

For the next three weeks, I barely held it together. I felt manic, excited, terrified, and unable to do anything except

---

11 This and the following texts/messages from here on out are the real messages. I save everything because I am a proud memory hoarder and I figured they'd come in handy some day.

obsess over when he'd come back. Then, finally, came his text: a simple "hi" with a caterpillar emoji (an inside joke). *Of course he just casually drops the caterpillar emoji after three months of not talking.* I was endeared by the implied familiarity. A couple of hours after the text, he was at my door smiling with a giant container of my favorite frozen yogurt. He'd planned this all out. I couldn't believe this was really happening.

We went for a walk and he explained his roller-coaster of emotion over the last few months. He admitted my letter changed everything for him and despite his ex being a good match on paper, spending time with her felt dull compared to me. I couldn't even dream up a better fantasy than hearing these words. The high was incomparable. He felt the same as I did about our magical connection! He understood! Everything felt right in the world. We meandered through the streets of our neighborhood and eventually began to hold hands. It was the happiest I'd felt in years.

But then, the sobering reality of trying to date a newly-single person hit. The next day, Miles woke up in a state of turmoil. He missed his ex. He felt guilty. He knew he made the right choice, but he was so confused. He needed time to sort himself out. He told me all of this without any filter because it had always been our style to be completely transparent with each other. I tried to support him. I told him (and myself) that it would just take time. And patience. And resilience. I coped by screenshotting countless Instagram quotes about loving someone and letting them go so they can come back to you. I filled pages and pages in my journal convincing myself that all this anxiety and turmoil would be worth it in the end. How could it not be? He *broke up with his girlfriend* for me!

But as weeks passed and then months, his internal storm only continued to rage and wreak havoc on my newly minted sense of okay-ness. Everything I'd learned in therapy and the 12-step group told me *girl, run* but the desire to have my fairy-tale fulfilled—to have the guy I loved come running back to choose me—ruled over all else.

Eventually, he sent a text that pushed me over the edge:

Some days I think about my wedding vows to you, and other times I'm not even sure we should be together at all.

This was perhaps the single most flagrant mixed message I'd *ever* received. It snapped me right out of my desperately-hoping-he-will-be-ready-soon stupor. I replied with a firm boundary: I could no longer talk to him until he made up his mind about me. I told him to only reach out when or if he was ever ready to date me. We stopped talking completely.

♡ ♡ ♡

Nine months later, he was back. He had missed me, he admitted. He had been waiting for the right moment to talk to me again. Once again, it felt like the circus had come to town for my wounded, waiting, hoping little heart. The manic high from being *remembered and missed* was back, a sugary surge of hope coursing through my veins. *Is he finally ready?*

No. He wasn't ready. He'd gotten back together with that same ex-girlfriend again, and then broken up again. He was still finding his footing, but said he wanted me in his life as something like a friend.

"We are *not* just friends," I rebuked, offended at the thought.

We agreed to stop talking again, but this time in a more mutual way. I left our brief meet-up hoping he'd eventually realize he was still in love with me.

♡ ♡ ♡

Six months later, he was back again, and at the most on-brand place ever: Burning Man. It was summer 2019 by this point and I was minding my own business at my camp, feeling rather proud of myself for all the growth I'd done in the past year. Then, in a very unexpected turn of events, a campmate told me the tidbit of information that was the beginning of my unraveling: *Miles came here looking for you*. There was that saccharine hope again. As much as I *knew* I should ignore this piece of information and move on like the *mature* woman I'd become, I did the complete opposite: I dressed in my sexiest white and gold bodysuit, hopped on my bike, and made a bee-line for Miles's camp.

I spotted him easily as I rode up and we immediately went in for a hug. The comfortable familiarity felt as addictive as ever. As soon as we separated, he said he had something for me. *He was expecting to find me here?!* He went rummaging in his tent and then handed me a small bag. Inside was a small pink and green rock that he'd picked up for me while traveling in Africa. A tiny but powerful gesture; I absolutely loved collecting rocks in foreign places and he knew this because he'd often tell me it was adorable when we'd traveled together. My heart fluttered as I remembered how it felt to be *known* by him. All semblance of boundaries and wisdom dissolved within me.

We got to talking and it was all inside jokes and knowing looks, like it always was with us. Eventually, we got onto the topic of dating. He asked me about my recent dating experiences and alluded to his. I felt like throwing up. *No, no, NO! This is all wrong!* People with our type of history don't discuss these things. No, I wouldn't settle for platonic niceties.

Not everyone gets the chance to actually have the real, blunt-question-asking conversation that they've played out in their heads for months (or years) with their on-and-off-situationship-or-maybe-soulmate. But I had the chance and I was going to take it. If not just for myself, then for everyone who has ever dragged their heart over coals for someone they never dated:

"Why aren't we together?" I blurted out, emboldened with frustration.

He laughed nervously and stammered through an explanation: he had just moved to San Francisco and, uh, still didn't really know what he wanted. I was armed for this answer and immediately shot back that we never even *tried*, and that I *knew* he had feelings for me because he couldn't stay away from me. He was caught off-guard by my bluntness and stumbled through another explanation: he didn't think he had romantic feelings for me anymore, and besides, he didn't ever think he'd make me truly happy. *Ouch.* But I wasn't ready to give up. Not after all this time. I needed answers.

"Then *why* do you keep coming back?!" I pressed. It felt *so* cathartic to finally voice my anguish to the real him rather than the him inside my head. The real him said he just *cared* about me and wanted me in his life. He didn't want to wake up in five years when I was married (to someone else) with a second baby on the way and feel like I was gone forever. Hearing about his "care" for me only upset me more—it felt like fuckboy behavior dressed up as nice-boy behavior. *No!* I was done with the mixed messages. I was done stewing in the swamp of will-he-won't-he torture. Now that I was in front of him, the fantasy of him was turning to dust and I saw him for who he was: a confused 27-year-old who had no idea what he wanted, least of all regarding me.

As this all dawned on me and I understood that the last several years of pining over him were for naught, I felt a seething anger building inside. I began to rip into him for torturing me with his indecision and for throwing a grenade into my life each time he came back. I told him he *had* to leave me alone because my heart couldn't take it anymore. As I said this, my quivering voice betrayed me; my hard determination finally cracked and revealed all of the softness I'd been hiding underneath the anger. Tears streamed down my face as fiery ash began falling on us from the nearby wooden art structure being burned. The sky was raining fire as the home I'd built inside of Miles furiously burned down. *What a fucking perfect metaphor.*

He immediately hugged me and apologized for upsetting me so much. I looked up and saw his eyes were glassy too. Seeing him upset only added to the bolus of grief that swelled in my chest because I *finally* understood the truth: the specific way he looked at me, his tears, the little gifts he brought for me—it all coexisted with his choice not to be with me. He was never going to date me. He was just going to keep coming back with mixed messages every three to nine months in perpetuity. His ambivalence would be the end of me if I didn't finally set (and abide by) a real boundary. So, I walked away from him that day, cried my eyes out, and then I opened my phone and blocked him before I could second-guess myself.

My Burning Man was ruined, in case you were wondering. I spent the rest of the week utilizing different spots on the ground to sob. At the end of the week, I finally carted my body, which had mostly devolved into an unshowered, crying machine, to a place called The Temple. The Temple was a beautiful, quiet place where it was customary to grieve loved ones.

On my solo bike ride over, a dust storm hit and I braced myself against the whipping winds and dust. As I saw the giant wooden posts of The Temple emerge in the distance, I noticed another person on a bicycle coming toward me, weathering the same storm. As the person neared, I saw the familiar red-tinted goggles. It was Miles. In a city of 80,000 people, of all the places to be in the seven miles of vast desert, Miles and I were somehow in the same 10-foot radius again.

He looked over at me and nodded his head as we rode by each other wordlessly.

How to Get Over Someone You Never Dated

Sometimes it's the "almost relationships" that break you more than anything else. Sometimes it's the stories that are abandoned mid-sentence that are the toughest to let go of.

Why? It's the seductive promise of potential. The unwritten future. The lingering what-ifs.

It's easy to get stuck in the mud of wondering what could have been. There was no real beginning, so there was no real end. It's a purgatory of unanswered questions. It's a painful abbreviation of something like love that never had a chance to grow into more.

There is a way out of this purgatory, though, and it involves a conscious effort to release the "what-ifs" and move forward with purpose. Here are a few ways to get over someone you never dated; you don't have to do all of them at once, but the more you do, the more successful you will be at moving on:

1. Stop Blaming It on Bad Timing

Blaming bad timing can be alluring because it means that perhaps in the future, there will be good timing and you two can finally be together! This feels like a surmountable hurdle—one worth waiting for—and that's why it can keep you stuck. The hard pill to swallow here is that in almost all cases, "bad timing" is really just a symptom of incompatibility and/or mismatched priorities.

The more-than-likely truth is that "bad timing" was masking other more uncomfortable realities like commitment issues, emotional unavailability, or a just-not-that-into-you situation. True, bad timing is possible, but it's generally a tangible obstacle that is resolved over time like temporary long distance or a very recent breakup. When bad timing is the real reason, it has a clear cause and does not persist endlessly.

Trust that the fact that you're not with this person is enough information for you to know it wasn't right. If it were right, you'd be together. So the faster you can accept that bad timing was very likely not the reason you're not with this person, the more easily you will be able to close this chapter and move on.

2. Stop Checking in on Them (and Remove Their Access to You)

"But he still watches my Instagram story..."
"But she still texts me sometimes..."
"But they posted ____, so it must mean ____..."

Nope. No more buts. These ways of casually keeping in touch with this person that you're still not over are keeping you stuck in the mire of false hope. Checking in on them and making assumptions about what their life is like now is slowing down your moving-on process. Allowing them to contact you or check in on your life at their convenience is keeping you from being able to fully heal and move on. It's like ripping the scab off a wound over and over. If you know they are watching your story, it's influencing what you post and it's keeping you tied to them.

When you have/had feelings for someone, it's really hard to move forward when some part of you is still clinging to what they're thinking about you. There is wisdom in the notion "out of sight, out of mind." Do yourself the favor of taking this person out of your sight for a while so that you can heal. Unfollow or block them so you aren't tempted to check up on them, or wonder if they're checking up on you. Blocking isn't mean, it's self-love and self-preservation. It doesn't have to be this way forever, only until you can get to a point where you truly feel like you've moved on.

3.   Let Yourself Be Sad

This sounds obvious, but it should not be overlooked. Sometimes the reason that you have a hard time getting over someone that you never really dated is because you don't give yourself permission to grieve them. You think, Well, we never dated so it would be pathetic to be really sad over it, right? *Not true.*

People that we never "date" can still have a significant effect on us. You don't need a label or a long time to develop strong feelings for someone. Gaslighting yourself into not feeling sad or lonely about this person is detrimental to your emotional health and only slows down your healing. So, let yourself be upset. Grieve the loss of this person as a romantic prospect, whether you knew them for two months or two years. Give yourself permission to feel however you are feeling, and eventually the emotions will lose their charge and you'll be one step closer to emotional freedom.

4. Make an Honest List of What You Liked and Disliked About Them

This accomplishes a couple of important things. First, by listing the good qualities, you can begin to understand what drew you to this person. In doing so, you'll likely realize that these qualities are not unique to this one person. They are not the last person on Earth that you can have silly inside jokes with, who is willing to take last-minute trips with you, who adores the way you look at 7 a.m., or who inspires you. You can (and will) find these qualities in someone else, and naming them helps you get better at finding them in people in the future!

Second, listing what you disliked, or what didn't work with this person helps to ground you back into reality. It helps you check yourself on who this person actually was, versus what you were projecting onto them. You might realize that you were a lot less compatible than you thought. Maybe their mediocre communication bothered you. Maybe you didn't like how they would rarely make time for you. Maybe the fact that they could never make a decision frustrated you. It helps to get this all out on paper, so you don't trick yourself into looking back on "what could have been" with rose-colored lenses. Reminding yourself of reality is a sobering but very effective way to move on.

♡ ♡ ♡

One last thing: remember that there is no "right" timeline for healing. You can take as long as you need to get over someone. Sometimes it takes a long time, maybe longer than makes logical sense to you. Sometimes it feels really traumatic. That's okay. Putting your heart on the line and developing feelings is never a shameful act. Getting over anyone, even an "almost relationship," is tough. But trust that you'll come out the other side. Trust that you will love again.

PART FOUR

Serial Dating

(30–31 years old)

Qualifications for dating me: "masculine," outdoorsy, really good with words, very obviously into me, states they are emotionally intelligent

CHAPTER NINETEEN

The Outside Help

I really didn't plan to become one of those charlatans who insisted Burning Man *changed* them, but there I was, changed. After that week, my whole relationship to grief changed; it felt like a floodgate had been irreversibly thrown open and all the grief stored within me came gushing out to be felt. I guess that's what happens when the fantasy of your "soulmate" realizing he's in love with you goes *poof* and you're left with everything you'd been unknowingly avoiding. Again.

I floundered for months as I realized just how high my grief had piled up in the past few years (or maybe my whole life?) and how little I had actually allowed myself to feel it. I'd just slapped yet another band-aid in the form of a person over my difficult emotions. *Gah! Foiled again by my own damn self!* So, I endeavored anew in fixing myself in every way I could find. I looked for new, better, deeper ways to heal. I was certain someone or something outside of me had the answers I was looking for. I was desperate to become "whole," and I would do whatever it took, even if that meant sobbing in front of near-strangers (the outside help) on a routine basis.

First, like many white women who have run out of other places to turn, I delved into the promising world of "manifesting." I wrote my Soulmate List, which included about 30 criteria that I wanted in my ideal partner. The criteria topping the list were: *emotionally intelligent and available, wants marriage and a family in the next five years, geographically available, consistent, makes me feel adored and safe, commits to me easily, physically masculine and tall, thoughtful, won't ever forget about me*. I even added some nice-to-haves like: *goes to bed at a normal hour, doesn't snore, as hungry or hungrier than me*. Then I did meditations where I pictured my future life with this mythical dream man. I envisioned him wearing a dark blue sweater and hugging me outside our home. I tried to conjure up the feelings of warmth and joy that I'd feel around him. But at the same time, I forced myself to "want it less" because per the rules of manifestation, wanting something too much creates desperation energy and blocks your manifestation from coming in. Ugh. So I tried, in my day-to-day life, to act as if everything had already been worked out for me. I tried to adopt the belief that he was out there making his way to me and I didn't need to worry. Ha! Me? Not worry? TALL ask.

Concurrently, I found a new Reiki practitioner in San Francisco whose website said she was good at "energetic cord cutting." This sounded perfect for me; I felt a (now frustrating) inextinguishable connection to Miles and I *needed* it to go away. I couldn't keep thinking about him every day and dreaming about him every night. On our third session, the Reiki healer led me through a shamanic journeying session where I dialogued with a three-year-old version of myself.

During this, without warning, I felt an all-encompassing wave of grief rise up from my stomach and I began to sob uncontrollably. But there was no reason or thought behind the sadness; it was pure emotion and it felt *old*, as if it had existed within me for decades. I had a few more sessions similar to this. I finally began to understand how maybe my sadness had very little to do with Miles, or any other guy for that matter.

Then (also concurrently), I joined an expensive women's group with the intention of learning how to embody my feminine energy. In my near-obsessive exploration of different dating coaches and advice, I had seen a lot about how feminine energy was the key to attracting (masculine) men. I had always felt a little uncomfortable with my own femininity and sexuality—on the inside, I still often felt like an awkward tomboy who just happened to have curves and wear floral dresses—so I was certain the feminine energy was my crucial missing piece.

When I first joined the group, it felt like a treasure trove of secrets that I couldn't unearth fast enough. What texts do I send to men to keep them interested? How do I curate my dating profiles to make men want to match with me? What do I wear to dates? What do I talk about? How do I come off as feminine and irresistible? The woman who led the group and the five group "mentors" seemed to have all the answers: get a professional photoshoot wearing dresses and a beaming smile for your profile, use *feeling* language with men, let them lead the conversation. Don't ask too many questions, let them plan the dates, wear something you feel sexy in on the date, do NOT offer to split the check, and definitely do not, by any means, be the first one to text after a first date. If a man is interested, he will follow up, they insisted. This all seemed a little Stepford-wives-y but I felt like I had nothing to lose by trying on a new way of dating (because my old ways had, ahem, not gone so well).

I had deleted my dating apps after Burning Man because I didn't want to mix dating and sobbing. But after about six months of intensive inner work, I started to feel that familiar, gnawing fear: *Lauren, you mustn't spend too long alone like this or else you'll get too old and the good ones will get snapped up and you'll be left alone just like you always feared.* This voice, plus encouragement from my woman's group to start dating lots of men, eventually won out and I got back on my least favorite carousel: OKCupid. It was not insanity, I told myself, because I had changed! I was trying the same thing, yes, but differently!

Off I went, applying all the strategies I had learned in the women's group and elsewhere. I went against my base instincts in conversations with men and started sending texts like this when a man would ask what I was up to:

I'm feeling so energized today! I just went on a walk and the sun felt so good on my skin and now I'm sipping my hot coffee and it feels so silky in my mouth and velvety as it goes down my throat mmmm :)

To be clear, the women's group leader stressed that we should not just apply "strategy," but actually *come from our own hearts* when interacting with men. I didn't really understand what this meant, so I kept trying to make my personality fit into this unfamiliar idealized-feminine-shaped mold. The idea of not asking questions and speaking in this flowery way felt very foreign to me. But I trusted the women's group with everything inside of me. The group leader and mentors had become my compass; the very direction I (still) lacked within myself.

It's not that seeking all this outside help was wrong, but I sought it at the expense of honing my own inner knowing. I thought I didn't have an intuition, or that it was broken. I thought my anxiety was something to be pushed aside and ignored. I thought I was inherently un-feminine and my only hope of learning was through women who had "figured it out." I was always on the edge of exasperation because it felt like love was being withheld from me for an unknowable reason. It felt like the more I wanted love, the less likely I would be to find it. It felt like everyone around me who had found a partner was somehow in on a secret that I hadn't yet uncovered.

But...I was certain that with my new thousands-of-dollars guidance, I'd eventually find the end of this mysterious love rainbow.

Thus began an era of serial dating at a higher volume than ever before.

CHAPTER TWENTY

The "Feminist" Who Thought Orgasm Reciprocity Was a Ridiculous Heteronormative Expectation

My first viable match under my new paradigm of dating was Gavin. We met early on in The Great 2020 Global Pandemic (you know the one), so we carefully navigated how to be within six feet of each other. We spent hours on the phone getting to know each other before meeting in person. I liked his deep voice and the funny little song clips he'd record for me. He was a whimsical, creative type who lived in an eclectic household of other 30-somethings in Oakland (where many creatives go after they get tired of and/or priced out of San Francisco). I quickly ascertained that he was very socially progressive, which felt novel to me at the time. He was a contrarian, had an opinion about everything, and was a self-proclaimed feminist. He was *very* different from anyone I'd ever dated and that alone felt like a promising re-entry into the dating world.

Our first several dates were dreamy, sunny days hiking to vista points in the Oakland hills where we pontificated endlessly. Dating during the pandemic meant our dates were not frequent and always outdoors, but I appreciated the chance to get to know him without any pressure or rush.

After several months, I invited him on a Fourth of July camping trip. On night two of the trip, we ended up sleeping together for the first time and it was about as okay as most first times are. The part that stood out was that after he was finished, he rolled over and fell asleep, without inquiring about me at all. *Hmm...that was kind of weird.* But I let it go since it *was* really late.

A couple of days later on the phone, I decided to set aside my "feminine chill" and politely ask him about it:

"Hey, so not a big deal, but I'm curious as to why you didn't try and reciprocate for me when we hooked up?"

He retorted with surprising defensiveness, explaining that it was unfair of me to assume he should just *know* to reciprocate. I was confused.

"What? Why wouldn't I want you to reciprocate?"

"Not every woman is comfortable with orgasm," he shot back, as if I was somehow insensitive for *even* bringing this up.

So, let me get this straight: we have mediocre-at-best tent sex and then afterward, suddenly he's concerned about my "orgasm consent"?! I explained to him that reciprocation has always been a normal thing in my sexual experiences; something I don't have to explicitly ask men for, especially *after* we've already had sex. This only agitated him more.

"Okay, well, first of all, that's *such* a heteronormative expectation," he started and continued to rant about my unfair expectations.

We continued back and forth for an hour until I realized we were never going to see eye to eye. If mansplaining could be personified...well...you get it. After that night, we never spoke again and I still wonder to this day about these women who are "not comfortable with orgasm."

CHAPTER TWENTY-ONE

The Three Months Out of a "Marriage" Guy Who Came on Way Too Strong

You know how you meet someone and it feels like they are what's been missing from your life the whole time? That's how I felt about Zach within days of matching with him on Hinge. He had piercing blue eyes and a knack for engaging questions, so almost immediately we found ourselves knee-deep in meaningful conversation. He didn't waste any time getting to the juicy, hard-hitting questions: *What was my perfect Saturday like? Did I want kids? What was I looking for in a partner? How did I feel about tantric sex?*

We soon realized how similar we were in terms of values and life goals. We both put a heavy focus on personal growth, active hobbies, frequent friend gatherings, and being judicious about a healthy work-life balance. He was, unsurprisingly, a software engineer. (I wasn't kidding when I said they are *everywhere*). He wanted kids too, maybe even sooner than I did. *Wow, what a nice change of pace, I don't have to worry about commitment issues with this guy!* The sex talk felt a little invasive so early on, but at this point in my dating career, I'd accepted that every guy on the apps would come with some slightly off-putting quirk—like discussing tantra before meeting in person—and I'd just have to deal. I reframed it as "open-mindedness."

The more we talked, the more we found in common. It became difficult to contain our excitement toward each other. I quietly thought he might be *the one*. In parallel, he started dishing out heavy praise to me:

I can't believe a woman like you exists; this is insane. It feels like you were engineered in a lab for me.

You are an incredible writer, please send me more of your articles.

I am so turned on all the time with you.

I felt so seen, it was intoxicating. This man adored my mind, my writing, and everything I'd told him about myself, all before even meeting me in person! He revealed early on that he was relatively fresh out of a five-year relationship, but that it had been "done" a year before they ended things officially. They'd had a "dead bedroom" the whole last year. He was still friends with his ex, but they had just fallen out of love over lifestyle differences. He was adamant that he'd fully processed everything already, and at the time I thought this meant he was exceptionally emotionally intelligent and highly skilled at processing difficult feelings (haha).

Hmm, this all seems reasonable, I convinced myself, as I careened off a cliff into an instant-relationship with him. There was this part of me, probably rooted in addiction, that *craved* this instant-relationship rush. I didn't understand how, in letting that part of me take the wheel, I was playing a major part in choosing situations that would later become painful. I prioritized the high of a man's intense affection over the wisdom of properly vetting his actions over time. So, of course, I conveniently ignored the guidance from my dogmatic women's group to take things slow and get to know a man over the course of months before deciding to be exclusive with him. I was the exception, I was sure of it! I had found my person!

Meeting Zach in person a couple of weeks after matching felt more like a formality than anything; when we met, we were both relieved that we found each other just as attractive in person. I liked that we had the pandemic as an excuse to become a couple instantly (COVID bubble and all that), but if I'm being honest I would have done that pandemic notwithstanding. I felt *crazy* about him, the type of ohmygodimgoingtomarryhim crazy that I'd only seen in movies; I could hardly sleep or eat (I would later learn this mania was *not* a good sign). He joked about me taking up half his closet after a few weeks of dating. I knew it wasn't really a joke, and I loved it.

But after a few visits to his place, I started to get the creeping feeling that I was filling a role that had been *very* recently vacated, so I inquired more about his ex. Well, they actually had a wedding, he admitted. But they never got *lawfully* married. *Uh, what?* So he was fake-married? He was barely three months out of a MARRIAGE?! I stalked his Instagram tagged-photos later and found full-on wedding photos from a couple of years prior. *Uh-oh.*

From there, our budding relationship began to unravel rather quickly. He kept trying to initiate sex by asking, "Orgasm time?" as soon as I arrived at his house. (Quite the contrast to the previous no-orgasm time with the last guy.) This clearly didn't work for me after only knowing him for a few weeks. Would it work on any woman? Who's to say. But he took my "slow" sexual pace personally. He couldn't understand why I wanted to wait to have sex, or why I felt a bit uneasy moving so quickly given his recent breakup-but-actually-fake-marriage-divorce, or why I didn't respond to his "Orgasm time?" question by ripping off my clothes immediately.

I felt him pull away, subtly at first and then obviously; my personal nightmare coming true, yet again. I asked about it and he seemed just as confused as I was. He explained that in theory, he was fine with being patient with sex, but in reality, he had lost his excitement for me and didn't know how to get it back. I was devastated. This (waiting for sex) had never been a problem for me before. How could he be *so* into me a couple of weeks ago and now cold and distant because I hadn't slept with him yet?

I'm embarrassed to admit that in a last-ditch effort to keep him, I offered to come over and just have sex with him if it was *such* a big deal. I figured it wasn't worth losing the man of my dreams just to wait a few more weeks to sleep together.

"What if I just like, wear a trench coat with nothing underneath and show up at your door?"

He declined, saying he didn't think our situation was resolvable (in retrospect, thank *god* he said no). I felt myself sink back into that dark, helpless place. I'd played all my cards and this man still didn't want me. We had a final closure conversation and he apologized profusely, promising this was his problem and he'd go to therapy. I hung up and deleted his contact from my phone, frustrated with myself for *yet again* falling for excited man babble[12] that ultimately meant nothing.

I started to wonder if maybe *I* was the common denominator here. Maybe I was attracting these burn-bright-burn-out situations because I was so desperate for love. But I wasn't ready or willing to take responsibility for my choices yet; going back for more swiping and manifesting was the much easier option. I fought my clawing urge to despair-delete all my dating apps and instead forced myself to just keep serial dating.

---

12 excited man babble (noun): when a man who you're getting to know acts extremely excited about you and talks about all the future plans he can't wait to do with you, but behind the scenes he probably doesn't mean it and is just swept up in the moment.

CHAPTER TWENTY-TWO

The Bearded Poet Who Forgot Who I Was After Three Dates

He had to push back our first date by 30 minutes because he was coming back from his poetry group. *Yum.* Men who are good with words are my kryptonite. During our video date, he showed me the well-manicured miniature jungle he had in his apartment. *And he takes good care of his plants?!*

He was witty in an understated, stoic way and I was immediately drawn to the way he'd take a beat before speaking. *So thoughtful,* I noted, proud of how much better I had gotten at choosing men. He told me how he'd dress up his adopted dog as a lion and tell little kids she was a *real* lion. We mused about funny costumes and bonded over our shared love of words.

We had a second video date that went equally well, which led to a third date where we met for a walk in Golden Gate Park with his dog. He knew an amazing amount about local history, so as we toured the park, he showed me a bunch of hidden areas I'd never been to. I was having a great time and was majorly crushing on him, with one exception: his very large dog was off-leash and kept running up to other dogs and scaring the bejesus out of people. He seemed to not mind and kept letting it happen. The more it happened and I saw the looks of terror and upset on people's faces, the more I cringed. *How unexpected for a guy who seemed so thoughtful!*

We ended the date with a hug. I had a feeling we might not see each other again and felt only lightly disappointed about it, especially given the weird dog behavior. Neither of us reached out again, and he faded into memory...

...until a few months later when I opened up Hinge and saw that he "liked" me. I used mostly the same pictures across my different app profiles so I thought this was one of those cheeky gestures when someone likes you *just* enough to come back around and say "hi" on a different app when they got bored with their other prospects. So I matched with him. Maybe he'd gotten his dog under control. He messaged me a flirty opener, the type of ice-breaker you say to someone you've never talked to before, and I realized... *Oh my god, he has no idea who I am!!! After THREE dates!*

I was aghast. I had to know if this could possibly be real, so I messaged him back and playfully mentioned our park date. He never responded. Then he unmatched me. *God, this again?!*

I was painfully reminded of my unrequited college crush, Noah, who'd *also* somehow forgotten about me after spending many hours together in social settings. Dating apps had this uncanny ability to continuously serve up my biggest insecurities, forcing me to face them head-on. Here was being *forgettable and forgotten,* hot and fresh!

No one wants toxic positivity—I get it—but I'm going to take a reframing stance here:

This "serving up all your insecurities" thing is actually an understated benefit of dating apps. It's kind of like going to shitty, painful therapy, where you undergo important personal growth fully against your will. I had a lot of flawed beliefs about myself—like being forgettable, being unattractive, being unfeminine—and using dating apps brought up these beliefs constantly. I had no choice but to confront them. Question them. Ask where they came from. Because they weren't *really* caused by these guys I hardly knew. They were deeper and required a slow and methodical dismantling. This dismantling was happening, almost imperceptibly, as I continued to date and confront, date and confront (and scream). I didn't understand this then (and I would have vehemently scoffed at the idea), but the apps were acting as an inadvertent battleground for my necessary evolution.

CHAPTER TWENTY-THREE

The Non–Monogamous Cofounder Who Really Wants Me to Follow Him on Instagram

I feel kind of sheepish asking you again, but I'd love to follow each other on Instagram, he'd texted after chatting for a few days.

At the time, I was flattered. We'd had a two-hour video date a couple of days prior with a rare, palpable chemistry that somehow translated through our phone screens. He was an engineer, had just cofounded a green tech[13] company, and was bursting with pie-in-the-sky ideas. He seemed to have at least three other startup potentials up his sleeve if this one didn't work out. The way he talked passionately about saving the environment was hot. He also had a "Partnership Vision" Google document link on his Hinge profile that he encouraged his dating prospects to read. Strange approach (slightly cringe?), but intriguing.

---

13 Green technology is an umbrella term that describes the use of technology and science to create products and services that are environmentally friendly.

I happily gave him my Instagram handle. The first time he asked to follow each other was after only a few Hinge messages, but I declined and explained my preference to get to know someone outside of a social media lens. But since he'd asked again and our virtual date went so well, I figured, why not?

A few days went by without any further communication. I then happened upon his profile on Tinder and saw that he listed "ENM" (ethically non-monogamous) in his bio. This was not in his Hinge profile or his "Partnership Vision" document. *This seems like a VERY critical preference to leave out of a Partnership Vision document?!*

I was looking for monogamy so I knew ENM was a deal-breaker for me. But I was still incredibly curious about his behavior. *Was he trying on different dating personalities on different apps? Was he just using dating apps to spread the word about his startup because this was San Francisco and that is a real thing that happens? Was he just collecting Instagram followers?* Out of curiosity, I took a deeper gander at his Instagram. My latter suspicion seemed to be confirmed—most of his followers and photo comments were 20- to 30-something women who appeared to be single, beautiful, and genuinely really cool. I smiled to myself and wondered if I'd ever hear from him again. I didn't, but I did later see him breezing through Golden Gate Park on a bike, surrounded by many fabulous-looking women. He later unfollowed me on Instagram.

CHAPTER TWENTY-FOUR
The Anti–Gentleman

Our pre-date conversation was filled with passionate discussion about our upcoming camping trips. It seemed I had finally found someone who liked backpacking as much as I did! He had the epic, mountain-filled Instagram photos to prove it. I couldn't wait to meet him and gush about each of our recent trips to Yosemite.

Our first date was at a fast-casual Mediterranean place in San Francisco. We perused the menu and laughed about both wanting the same dish. We also agreed about how incredible the frozen yogurt with Baklava toppings looked. *Same taste! Cute!* He reached the register first and ordered his salad. When the person at the register asked, "Anything else?" he made it clear he was only ordering and paying for himself. *Okay, no big.* It felt nice and gentlemanly when men offered to pay for a first date, but it wasn't something I felt entitled to.

As we ate, I noticed that he seemed generally disinterested in being gentlemanly in *any* way whatsoever. He poured himself water, but not me. He made very few attempts to ask me anything about myself. He mentioned he had little interest in traveling the 40 minutes from the small town where he lived to San Francisco very often. It became clear neither of us were into it. But then came the grand finale! As I mentioned, we'd waxed poetic about the delicious Baklava fro-yo. My eyes lit up when he brought it up again.

"I'm going to go in and get some," he told me after we'd finished our salads. For some reason, at that moment, perhaps because frozen yogurt runs like $4, I guessed he might get me some too. He came back out with a single, huge cup of frozen yogurt, practically overflowing.

"Wow they sure give you a lot!" he bemused, eyes wide.

"Haha...yeah they sure do!" I said, waiting to see if he'd offer to share or acknowledge *anything* about this very one-sided yogurt situation. Neither the offer nor any acknowledgment ever came. He sat in front of me polishing off his tower of frozen yogurt for six minutes, saying almost nothing. I'm usually quite conversational, but at this point I was so turned off that I let the silence linger during the longest six minutes of my life.

As soon as he finished, he got up and said he'd better be going. About 37 minutes of the date had elapsed at this point. I could not wait to be done. We didn't hug, but instead just turned and walked in opposite directions. We both swiftly unfollowed each other on Instagram, never to speak again.

CHAPTER TWENTY-FIVE

The Stands-Me-Up then Keeps-Coming-Back-Around Guy

Everyone who has used dating apps has probably experienced some iteration of this: a person matches with you, chats you up, asks you out (or you ask them out), then when it comes time to actually meet up, they go dark. Or worse, they confirm the date and then stand you up.

Enter: Tom. I had seen him repeatedly on OKCupid over the years, but never felt inclined to match with him. Eventually, some combination of desperation, boredom, and hope pushed me to finally return his bid of interest. After a few messages, I was happy I did; I enjoyed our banter and wondered why I passed him over all those times. He quickly asked me out on a coffee date. *Maybe this is fate and he's actually the person the Universe keeps trying to introduce me to!*

When the day rolled around for the date, he was suspiciously quiet. I momentarily considered that he might possibly not show up for our date, but no, that was ridiculous. *That's just your stupid anxiety you silly bitch.* Well, my anxiety was right. When I showed up to the cafe—which, luckily, was right around the corner from my house—he wasn't there. *Okay, no problem, I'm always early.* Five, ten, fifteen minutes passed, and still no sign of him. I bit back my ego and sent him a text asking if he'd remembered that we had a date (that, let me emphasize, we'd planned the DAY before). He replied apologizing profusely; he had forgotten about it.

I felt hot anger flush my cheeks, followed by shame. I had been forgotten about. There was that belief again: *I am easily forgettable.* Some young part of myself stirred inside of my chest, ready to scream or cry or claw at him. But I pushed that part down and replied with a watered-down version of how I was actually feeling because, even after being stood up, I still wanted him to want me (*sigh*). And it worked; he asked if we could meet the following morning and *promised* he'd show up. I told myself I was forgiving enough to let this go (hello again, Cool Girl) and I agreed to the date.

He did show up and the date was rather unremarkable. He was awkward in person, but a bit cuter than his pictures let on. The latter made me feel way more drawn to him than I should have been, given the situation. To end the date, we walked a few blocks as I headed to work, and he, back home (he was unemployed at the time, which made the initial date-forgetting even more egregious). While walking, he trailed behind me one to two feet the whole time. I kept slowing down my gait to try and match him, but it was a lost cause. We finally parted with an unpleasant, stiff hug. Even after ALL OF THAT, a majority part of me hoped he'd ask me out again.

He didn't ask me out again. Not in that same year, at least. I didn't hear from him after that date and I was forced to process all the shame and desperation that followed. *This guy stood me up and then took me on a super awkward date and I still needed him to ask me out again to feel okay?!* The feeling of being rejected by someone who you weren't even that into in the first place is a truly self-esteem-shattering experience.

♡ ♡ ♡

A little over a year later, still knee-deep in my serial-dating desperation phase, I set up a Facebook Dating profile. Within a few days, I saw a "like" from Tom. I matched with him for a myriad of bad reasons, the main one being curiosity. Here's one thing you should know about me: my need to *understand* trumps literally everything else. I wanted to understand why he acted the way he did. I thought that maybe by understanding, that young, hurting part of myself would feel less rejected.

When I reminded him that he stood me up the year prior, he said he didn't remember doing that, but he apologized anyway. He asked if he could make it up to me by taking me on a park picnic date. I DON'T KNOW WHY I SAID YES, BUT I DID. He suggested a park near him, on the opposite side of town. I asked if we could possibly meet somewhere more in the middle. He never responded. That same red-hot anger rose up in me. *How did I let this happen AGAIN?!* I wasn't usually one to tell guys off, but there was no way I was going to let this one go. After about a week, when I was certain he'd ghosted me, I wrote up a sternly-worded reply explaining that his dating behavior was hurtful and that I hoped, for the next woman's sake, he learned to communicate better. He wordlessly unmatched me within the hour.

♡ ♡ ♡

Another year and a half later, I got a random text on an alternate texting app from a number I didn't recognize: **Are you going to burning man this year?**

I replied: **Who is this?**

They replied: **tom**

I had no idea who this could be, so I replied again: **Do you know me?**

No reply came, but then I took a closer look at the tiny profile picture and the recognition hit me: it was *that* Tom. The one who had stood me up, faded out, came back, disappeared, unmatched me, and now was apparently back again. *Ew.* I deleted the chat. Then, another six months later he friend-requested me on Facebook. *Okay, something is really off with this guy.* I ignored it again, flabbergasted at this guy's audacity and a little creeped out.

Soon after all this, I went on a weekend cabin trip with a newer group of friends and the topic of dating apps came up one evening. We were trading horror stories and strange experiences, and since the Tom saga was fresh on my mind I chimed in with the story. When I mentioned his name and how he messaged me on multiple different platforms months after he ghosted, another girl was like, "WAIT! That happened to me too!!" We realized we'd been talking to the same Tom.

Apparently, I'd had it pretty easy because his opening line to her was a question about her opinion of circumcision. When she replied asking if he was serious, he replied with a selfie in his anti-circumcision shirt (yes, really, she kept a screen-shot) and said he was of smaller-than-average size but he knew how to use it. When she responded, *obviously* creeped out, he insulted and unmatched her. Then a month later, he tried to match with her again on a different app and *then* requested to follow her on Instagram. *What kind of woman does he think this unhinged, predatory dating strategy would work on?!*

Anyway, Anti-Circumcision Tom was not my soulmate.

CHAPTER TWENTY-SIX

The Effusive Frenchman Who Demanded His Gifts Back

We met for the first time in an airy, bright, Turkish restaurant and as we ordered appetizers he made it known he was immediately smitten.

"I made this for you; a flower almost as beautiful as you," he purred in a thick accent as he handed me a small rose he'd woven from a palm frond. He sprinkled in lots more praise and affection as our date went on. On several occasions, he paused to literally just stare at me in adoration. It felt a little strange, but also refreshing? Most men in San Francisco were much more guarded, only showing affection and clear interest after a few drinks. Here I finally had clear signals!

For our second date, he picked me up and took me to a fancy dinner in the adjacent town where he lived. As we spooned up couscous and sipped rosé, I started to notice some possessive and off-putting comments:

"Oh, was that your other boyfriend?" or "You never call me, are you too busy on other dates?"

He'd say "Just kidding," but I could sense an air of discontent underneath. As our date progressed, I realized I was way less into him than he was into me and I'd need to backpedal kindly out of this situation. Plus we'd been on the date for many hours, so I let him know I was tired and would like to head home. He agreed, no problem. But on the drive, I realized we were going the opposite way of home.

"We're just going to stop by my house really quick," he explained. "I have something for you." I was annoyed, but it wasn't much of a detour. *Fine*. At his house, he gave me the tour and then handed me a small jewelry box: my gift. It was a small pair of teal and silver earrings, my favorite jewelry colors. I forced a smile and thanked him as sweetly as I could muster, not quite sure how to receive this gift from a man I hardly knew. He then commented on me still having my shoes on and asked in an annoyed tone if I "just wanted to leave now."

"Um...yeah? I thought we were just stopping by for a minute?"

"Okay, we can go, let's go," he reluctantly agreed, and took me home.

After that date, we talked very sporadically and I eventually let him know I wasn't feeling like I had time to go on more dates with him. This was my mistake—doing the classic "nice let-down" rather than just being fully honest that I didn't want to date *him* anymore, at all, ever.

Months went by. I'd get a text from him every now and then. A happy birthday. A "hope you have fun in Europe!" nicely. I'd reply politely, and that was it. One day, he asked to have a phone call to "catch up" after we'd both gone on Europe trips. I realized I had to really cut the cord this time. I typed up a text explaining clearly that I didn't want to pursue anything further with him and that a "catch-up" phone call might send the wrong message.

He then exploded on me, sending me a barrage of texts, accusing me of leading him on for months, lying, and callously hurting him. I apologized for not being more clear and left it at that. He continued to berate me. We hadn't meaningfully talked or seen each other since the second date four months prior so I was shocked he felt so angry, but I didn't think it was worth arguing, so I stopped replying.

From there, he sent me weekly texts demanding that if I *really* cared and was *really* sorry, I should give all of his gifts back. I could leave them in a bag for him to pick up, he instructed. *First of all, "gifts," plural? Is he counting that palm frond rose in there? Is this guy for real?* I felt a little scared at this point because he knew where I lived. After the third angry text, I blocked him and hoped he wouldn't show up on my doorstep one day. He never did, but some time later someone wrote my phone number in multiple men's public restrooms with "call me baby" scrawled next to it. I have no proof it was him, but I have my suspicions.

The Commodification of Love (and How to Escape It)

Sometimes I like to imagine the conversations that happen in meetings at Match Group, Inc. (who, by the way, owns Hinge, Tinder, OkCupid, Match, and several other dating apps). I picture a group of employees gathered around a whiteboard, brainstorming about the question written on the board:

"How do we make more money?"

On the board already are several bullet-pointed ideas:
- *Remove more free filters (can we remove age? Distance?)*
- *Limit swipes per day and charge for extra (10–15 free swipes?)*
- *FY 2023 theme: Increase user desperation = increase revenue per user*
- *More in-app ads—increase to 1 ad / swipe?*

Someone in the back excitedly raises their hand with a new idea. "Ooh, how about we show them a curated batch of the most popular users each day, but only let them match by paying?"

The group loves this idea! It's perfectly in-line with the year's theme of increasing user desperation to facilitate more revenue.

♡ ♡ ♡

I use this maybe-not-that-far-from-the-truth fictional scenario to illustrate a couple of very real truths. First, if there is any way to make money off something, it will eventually be monetized. Second, humans in general are highly motivated by love and by fear. So, by marrying those two truths, there emerges a pervasive modern phenomenon: the commodification of love.

This phenomenon started well before dating apps, but much like the internet did for...well...everything, dating apps catalyzed a new on-demand economy for love. We're a swath of generations grown accustomed to ordering, listening, streaming, swiping, watching, and liking through our phones. If we can order a ride across town, get Pad Thai delivered at 1 a.m., and rent a vacation home through an app, it follows that we should apply that same on-demand economy to love. Right?

The apps gave us this new, exciting medium to feel like we could take tangible action toward finding love. Whereas before we had to depend on meeting people through friends, at work, or through pure serendipity, now there was a shiny collection of eligible singles waiting just a swipe away. At first, of course, it was mostly free. But over time, as both our illusion of choice and, paradoxically, our fear of not finding the right person grew, money entered the equation. Dating apps had us by the heart and they knew it. Slowly but surely, we started being sold the idea that money would get us closer to love. Want more swipes? Want more curated matches? Want access to this "exclusive" dating app? Want better filters to sort by? Want to be seen by more potential matches? Pay up! After all, what's a little money in comparison to finding your soulmate?

Even if you manage to avoid spending money on dating apps, there are countless other people and businesses waiting to capitalize on your desire for love and/or your fear of ending up alone. There are dating coaches selling "How to Get the Guy / Girl" courses. There are manifestation programs that will teach you how to believe your way into a relationship. There are feminine energy "boot camps" that promise, in eight weeks, to teach you the tried-and-true secrets to effortlessly magnetizing your dream man. There are men's coaches who promise to teach the charisma and confidence required to attract women (pickup artistry being one of the more toxic examples). There are even exorbitantly priced matchmakers for busy professionals who don't have time to date, or desperate singles who feel they've exhausted all their other options. (Did you know professional matchmakers, on the low end, cost $7,000 for three dates?! I was one of those desperate singles who came very close to spending this much on a matchmaker.)

The success of all of these people, businesses, and services depends on you believing that someone else has the answers. They depend on you feeling like there is something in you to be fixed, or some secret that needs uncovering, or some strategy that needs to be learned. They depend on you not trusting yourself. They depend on you feeling like you're getting too old, or that time is running out, or that all the "good ones" are getting snatched up. They depend on you believing that love can (directly or indirectly) be bought.

As a late-20s and early-30s woman who wanted love more than anything but couldn't seem to find it despite my best efforts, I was the perfect target for all of this commodification. And I wasn't alone; I was part of the near-bottomless demographic for this love economy: 20, 30, 40, and even 50-something singles who, deep down, fear that they might be forever alone. This fear caused me to use the dating apps like my life depended on it. To go on hundreds of dates and repeatedly fall into "last man on Earth" syndrome: every time a promising dating prospect or short-term relationship fell through, I'd feel, despairingly, like it was my last chance at love. This fear caused me to seek outside help at every turn, to try every single new therapy or dating coach or strategy I could find. And with each new outside voice, I became more dependent on the exterior. I moved farther and farther away from my inner knowing.

That's the destructive part about applying a capitalistic mindset to something as pure and intangible as love: it convinces us, in our most vulnerable moments, that what we want is behind a paywall. It contaminates a complex and sacred human experience with flavors of transactional urgency and never-enoughness. Under this model, we are encouraged to seek endlessly, to consume, to think someone better is just around the corner, to stay on the carousel of New! More! Different! We are encouraged to always ask someone else if we are "doing it right." We are almost never encouraged to slow down, get quiet, go within, or hone our intuition and knowing. But the truth, that so many of us can't see underneath the trappings of the love economy, is that we each have an innate, quiet wisdom already within us. It comes standard-issue with being a human.

The tricky thing about this innate wisdom is that it's often quieter than what's coming at us from the outside. It's less rushed, more subtle. It's less "quick fix" and more "lifelong journey." Ironically, sometimes we do need some outside guidance to help us see through all the fear and anxiety that can parade as truth. I definitely didn't need most of the external chatter that I took in over the years, but what did make a real difference for me was the guidance I received in confronting my own problematic dating behaviors. After trying to find the shortcut to love by using "man magnetizing" strategies in my women's group (to no avail), the leader of the group asked me if I was finally ready to address my love addiction. I stubbornly agreed and began the humbling process of unlearning the patterns that I always thought were just inherently "me": the obsessing, the ruminating, the pining, the crippling fear of being alone, the anxiety, the desperation, the fantasizing-as-a-coping-mechanism, the trying to skip steps and jump into a relationship right away. Of course I couldn't hear my intuition underneath all of that.

I never needed the strategies or the secrets or the boot camps or to go on just one more date. The whole time, all I needed was to clear out the fear-grown thicket that blocked me from my own eternal truth. When I was finally able to hear that quiet voice, it had a simple message for me: you are meant for love and you can trust in that. There was no doubt, no complication. No "you need to fix these three things about yourself and then you'll find love."

There was such a grounded clarity to this voice that I knew it was the truth. I knew I could trust it. That is, trust myself.

Each person's wise inner guidance has a specific texture, unique to only them. But you'll know it when you hear it because it's not rushed or cutting or militant. It's not the urgent voice telling you to do more, more, more. It's not the fearful, catastrophizing voice that pushes you to do things that tire out your soul in the name of some nightmarish future you couldn't bear to live. It's not the harsh, judgemental voice that tells you to change yourself or to settle for mediocrity lest time tick away and leave you behind. No, the wise inner voice is timeless and patient. It validates your existence and the yearning in your chest. It reminds you, tirelessly, that everything you deeply desire, you desire for a simple reason: you are meant for it, and it is meant for you. It leads you, often magically, to the people and places and things that feel like warm honey spreading through your veins.

Learning to trust your own inner guidance is the necessary antidote to commodification because it's free. It requires nothing of you except your priceless dedication to your own fulfillment. The love economy will continue with or without you, but you always have the choice to take a hard left turn away from it all. You always have the choice to not allow anyone or anything to capitalize on the unique timing of your life. You have the choice to reject the idea that you should be or have or do anything by a particular age, and instead to trust that you are right on time for your own life.

PART FIVE

Pattern Break

(31 years old–Present)

Qualifications for dating me: thoughtful, consistent, curious, passionate, kind, wants a family, lives with purpose and integrity, *very* into me

CHAPTER TWENTY-SEVEN

The Guy Who Thought Backpacking Was Taking a Jansport Into the Woods

It was Spring 2021 and I'd recently recommitted myself to the apps. I hadn't actually deleted them this time around (because my women's group said that was immature behavior), so recommitting looked like getting professional photos taken for my profile(s) and being *much* more strict about my filtering criteria. No more lukewarm or inconsistent men! No more falling for cheap compliments! No more sticking around for hot guys who never asked me questions! *Definitely* no more getting involved with men who weren't clear about wanting marriage and kid(s) in the future. Though these new and improved criteria meant *much* slimmer pickings, the apps had this way of dangling very promising prospects just out of my reach so that I'd maintain a glimmer of hope and keep swiping. The Hinge "Standouts" feature had recently been launched and was extremely effective at said dangling; every day it would show me 10 of the most popular men in my area and to have a chance at matching with them—you guessed it—I'd have to pay. To sweeten the deal, Hinge gave me one free "rose" a week to send to these standouts (*so generous*). I always sent my weekly free rose. I never got a match from it. But (this is the addictive part) I felt like, eventually, with enough persistence, I'd win the man lottery.

I was spending a *lot* of time on the apps—easily multiple hours per day—because I didn't feel I could leave my love life up to the "mysterious bidding of the Universe." I was only a few months out from my 32nd birthday and I felt like time was chasing me. I tried not to do the math, but the simple arithmetic was hard to ignore: if I met a partner at 32, we'd likely date for at least two years before getting engaged. Then, probably, add another year before marriage which would put me at 35. Then, add in a year for enjoying marriage without children (36) and add some indeterminate amount of time for getting pregnant during the "geriatric years" (37? 38?!). This was all assuming I *even* met someone in the next year. *Fuck. Fuck!* How was I supposed to remain calm and not desperate given this timeline? I had never felt "baby-crazy" but I *was* a planner, and staring into the dark abyss of the unknown future as a single woman in her 30s who was pretty sure she wanted children was...terrifying. Nevertheless, I tucked all of this away as a "later problem" and persisted.

After a season of disastrous dating experiences, Dylan was the first guy I felt excited about (and really attracted to) in a long time. After our first date—dinner at a lush, plant-filled patio restaurant in the Castro district—he took my hand and kissed me on a street corner. I hadn't kissed on a first date in ages, but *hot damn* did I feel a rare chemistry! As we waited for our respective Ubers home, we snuck into an alcove between restaurants and made out. The red lights from the Chinese place behind us set our cheeks aglow and seared the moment into my brain as the certain *start of something.*

Our next many dates consisted of hours spent lying side by side in Golden Gate Park, baring our souls to each other. We talked about our dating journeys and dreamed up future camping trips while flirting shamelessly. He made me laugh and expressed easy affection toward me. It felt uncomplicated. We seemingly had physical, intellectual, and emotional chemistry—a combination that always seemed to elude me. I was smitten.

But as the weeks went by, I (sadly) started to notice some habits and admissions by him that gave me pause. First was his admission that he didn't have many friends nearby, and the ones he did have "kind of sucked." When I asked what he meant, he said that he was friends with a couple in which the boyfriend physically abused the girlfriend, but nothing was being done about it. *Umm...excuse me?*

Second was his opening up about some adolescent experiences that had negatively affected him. He thought they contributed to some social struggles he had, and in a deeper way, how he interacted with me as a romantic partner. I asked if he'd ever looked into any form of therapy, or would look into it in the future. He said no, he didn't think he needed it. *Sigh.* The concept of acknowledging you have issues negatively affecting you but then being unwilling to work on them felt *so* foreign to me.

Unfortunately, this was a very common experience for me and many of my female friends: dating men who had not done any work on themselves and didn't really care to. Dating men like this often meant grappling with their low emotional intelligence, lack of self-awareness, non-existent coping skills, or emotional unavailability. From experience, these men would throw it in reverse and back themselves out of relationships without warning, ghost, have angry outbursts, or admit they haven't cried since age 12 (yes, actually). I'd mostly accepted it as the status quo, but I was frustrated by it because, as a straight woman, it was either date men or be alone.

I didn't know how to handle this emotional crevasse between myself and many of the men I dated. Encouraging someone you're newly dating to look into therapy felt condescending and inappropriate, but trying to build a relationship with someone despite glaring unresolved issues felt risky. I wasn't asking for perfection, but I desperately wanted to date an equal; someone willing to work on themselves for their own benefit and the benefit of their future relationship. Since I eventually wanted kids, I couldn't help but think about how these men would be as fathers. I saw in myself how emotional immaturity in a caretaker could cause silent damage. If I wanted to shield my own kid(s) from that, I'd have to choose wisely. Because how a man treated me (and himself) was how he would treat our children. I tucked that undeniable truth away as a reminder to myself every time I had the maybe-I-can-deal-with-this concessionary thoughts that tended to erupt when I was feeling hopeless.

Back to Dylan: I felt torn. I really liked him but I didn't want to get myself into yet another disappointing one-to-four-month "relationship" that was doomed to fail. His self-admitted "issues" were the type of information I'd learned to PAY ATTENTION TO after so many experiences of over-looking clear compatibility issues. I decided to make a big bold mental note of all of this and continue to see him...for now. Maybe I was being too hard on him.

After about two months of dating, I invited Dylan on a camping trip in Big Sur with some friends. We had talked about our shared love for camping and backpacking on our first many dates, so I was really excited to bring him to one of my favorite places on the gorgeous California coastline. The afternoon before leaving, we were sitting on a blanket in the park and he asked me what he should bring camping. I told him to just bring the stuff he uses for backpacking—something he said he did regularly.

"Oh, you know, just the usual. Sleeping bag, sleeping pad, warm clothes, food for a couple days."

"Oh...shoot. I don't have any of that..." he admitted sheepishly.

I was puzzled, and he seemed...equally puzzled. I had assumed that as self-proclaimed denizens of the outdoors, we had the same definition of backpacking: putting every-thing you need for many days and nights in a giant backpacking backpack and going deep into the wilderness. At that moment, I realized I must have assumed incorrectly. I asked quizzically what he meant when he told me he back-packed. His answer was...not what I expected:

"Well you know, I just put some stuff in my backpack and go for a hike."

"Like a regular backpack? Like a Jansport?"

"Yeah, just my regular backpack."

I giggled at the misunderstanding and then tried to be patient about his major lack of preparedness that I'd just become aware of. I scrambled that evening to see if any friends had extra camping gear and luckily found most of what Dylan would need. I told him I'd bring some snacks and dinner for one night for us, but he should bring food to feed himself for other big meals, and possibly some extra if he wanted to contribute to the communal vibe (my friends and I usually shared snacks).

Once we arrived in Big Sur, it was very clear that Dylan had never actually camped before. (For anyone who doesn't camp, no judgment! Everyone starts somewhere. But the *worst* thing to do is to pretend like you know what you're doing, not ask for help, and then show up unprepared.) When it came to setting up the tent and campsite, Dylan stared at me blankly and made little effort to help. He then revealed that he brought a light jacket that was definitely not going to keep him warm enough. In terms of food, he brought only granola bars and trail mix for the whole weekend. After setting up camp, he was immediately too hungry to be sated by said paltry snacks, so we had to leave camp to search for food to sustain him for the weekend (not an easy task; Big Sur is remote with no cell phone service). We found a tiny market and he bought several over-priced ham sandwiches.

At this point, I was majorly turned off. The ick started to worm its way into my body. I was flabbergasted that I had to explain to a 30-year-old man that granola bars and trail mix were not enough sustenance for a weekend. I felt frustrated that he hadn't just told me the truth about his lack of camping experience (I would have happily helped him prepare weeks before the trip), and doubly frustrated that I had to hold his hand through something as basic as bringing enough food for himself.

My attraction to Dylan swiftly died that weekend and never recovered. The camping trip was the final straw, but altogether his actions painted a picture of a man who lacked the self-awareness and thoughtfulness I needed in a partner. I ended things over the phone a couple of days later. *Maybe I should try dating older men, they've GOT to be better.*

CHAPTER TWENTY-EIGHT

The Dueling 40-Somethings

I opened up all of my various dating apps and slid the age-range clickers from 38 up to 40. I considered for a second and then clicked up to 42. I was 32 at the time, so dating 10 years older felt right on the edge of my level of comfort, but I went with it anyway. Within a few days, I had an influx of new, older matches. It felt very exciting at first because I'd swiped some of the apps dry (a truly awful feeling) and rarely saw anyone new. But I quickly realized that age does not magically make a man more mature or compatible with me. I matched with several new men in their 40s who salaciously asked for selfies, inquired about the color of my underwear, tried to convince me to date them despite being very recently divorced, or who had zero conversational skills. I felt deflated.

But then! A treasure amidst the sea of riffraff: Julian. He was 40, bearded like Oscar Isaac, and had photos of himself volunteering with children on his Bumble profile. We matched and shortly thereafter began one of those promising conversations where you're both excitedly asking and answering multiple questions in lengthy replies. He told me about his dream to visit all the natural rock arch formations in the United States because they just felt *so magical* to him. He had recently sold the public education startup he'd founded and was dreaming up what he wanted to do next. I was so endeared by his energetic, optimistic spirit and devilishly handsome smile. I finally had the self-esteem to believe I was worthy of a man like this.

After a few days of chatting, he let me know a piece of disappointing news: he actually lived in Los Angeles and was just in San Francisco visiting family when we matched. I wasn't interested in long distance, but we both seemed enamored with each other enough to continue talking. The paragraphs-long texting led to weekly video dates. After every date my cheeks hurt from smiling and he'd sign off by saying something like, "You've been the highlight of my day."

So when, on one of these video dates, he mentioned he was planning to visit San Francisco again soon, I practically fell out of my chair in excitement. A few weeks later, we had our first in-person date at my favorite cafe in the city: The Mill. As I rounded the corner and we made real-life eye contact for the first time, his hazel-green eyes lit up and he wrapped me in the warmest hug. *Oh my god, he's so hot in person! I'm so fucked.* As he pulled away and looked at me, his first words were: "We have the same color eyes!" We then both admitted to feeling nervous but soon fell into easy laughter as we sipped our $6 coffees and meandered through the blocks of picture-perfect Victorian houses. He even brought a thoughtful little gift for me because my birthday was the following week. At the end of the date, he looked me in the eyes and said, "I had the most amazing time with you," before kissing me sweetly. I left the date in a euphoric dream-state.

We had a second, even *more* magical date that same week at the botanical garden in Golden Gate Park. He brought a picnic and wine and mentioned that he couldn't have too much wine or he'd say things meant for a ninth date rather than a second date. *Ahhh, he's feeling it too!* As we wandered through the flora of the world, I felt myself uncontrollably falling for him. He was just such a *man* with his gray-flecked beard and business ideas. We talked about the long-distance hurdle and he said it was very possible that his new career ventures could bring him back to the Bay Area. Or possibly New York. But I tried to ignore that second, way-too-far-away option. As the date wrapped up and we walked together to the train he'd be taking to the airport, he said he couldn't wait to visit again. He wanted to show me how *very* into this (me) he was. I watched his train roll away until I couldn't make out his head in the foggy window anymore. My heart was bursting at the seams with hope.

In the following month, we continued to have weekly video dates but he didn't seem to be pushing our relationship forward. This was not what I expected after the whirlwind week of romance we'd had. Sometimes he'd go three, four, or even five days without responding to a text. But he always would eventually reply, and with that same enthusiastic fervor that I'd fallen for in the first place. *Maybe I'm just being paranoid.* It felt like a familiar pattern—my anxiety would slowly climb in the silence when I hadn't heard from him in a while, and then it would go *poof* the moment I saw his name pop up on my phone. Finally getting that text from him was sickeningly euphoric and eerily reminiscent of the hot and cold men of my 20s. I decided that I was putting too much pressure on this burgeoning relationship, so I convinced myself to go on other dates.

♡ ♡ ♡

Enter: Brett. We matched on Tinder during an afternoon when I was feeling particularly social. Within an hour of matching, we chatted on the phone and connected so well that we decided to go on a date later that evening. Just before hanging up, the topic of age came up and I realized his Tinder profile had no age listed. I asked how old he was and he hesitated for a moment before saying he was 43. I asked why he didn't list his age. He said he felt young at heart and didn't want his age to dictate who he matched with. *Ahh, the classic "age is just a number" adage.* I teased him a little about it but ultimately decided there was no harm in his approach. And besides, he was only one year outside of my age filters. Maybe age *was* just a number.

On that first date, I brought a bottle of Pinot Noir and we shared it clandestinely inside an enclosed Ferris wheel car. Our knees bumped together as we rattled over the landscape below and talked about our various personal-growth journeys. He was charming in that 40s-guy way—humble, quietly confident, and very easy to talk to. We touched on the topic of age again and he went into more detail; he felt much younger than his age and preferred to date younger women rather than women his own age. He related to their carefree and laid-back energy more.

This type of age preference made me uncomfortable; I was acutely aware of the phenomenon of older men dating much younger women because they just "feel more on my level." It was all over the place in Hollywood and seemed, to me, to perpetuate an unhealthy obsession with youth and beauty. I'd encountered this once before myself, when I was 26 and on a date with a guy in his mid-30s who confidently asserted he *only* dated women in their mid-20s and below (I ended it after that). Being that younger woman is flattering in the moment, but what happens when you age out of their preferred age range? I mentally noted Brett's age preference as "potentially problematic" and promptly pushed it out of my mind when he politely asked to kiss me. It was a really good kiss.

He walked me home and hinted that he *really* wanted to do more than just kiss me. I told him that I move slowly and he'd have to be patient. He respected my boundary and kissed me goodbye. I walked inside my front door feeling surprisingly good. *Look at me, dating two cool older men!* I invited Brett to a party at my house a week later for our second date (bold, I know). We ended up canoodling on the couch for much of the party and my friends mentioned it seemed like he was really into me. I was starting to like him more, too, and felt excited to see what developed. As the party wrapped up and I went upstairs to bed, Brett again tried to make a move on me. I rebuffed him and said I needed more time to get to know him before we got sexual. He was understanding and respectful and we agreed to see each other again soon.

♡ ♡ ♡

It had been over a month since Julian had visited from LA, and he'd still made no mention of plans to visit again. I was confused. He was so adamant about coming back to San Francisco when we last saw each other. *Was that just excited man babble? What about the thoughtful gifts? Why did he keep scheduling video dates? Should I go visit him?* I was leaving for a trip to Europe soon, so I tabled my confusion and kept showing up to the video dates with a beaming smile. I figured he'd probably bring up visiting again once I was back from Europe. His birthday was coming up soon, so I spent my rumination energy coming up with a heartfelt gift idea. I decided to write him a poem about our dreamy time spent together.

On the day I left for Europe, both Julian and Brett sent me very sweet bon-voyage messages. Brett referred to me as his "favorite moon lady" (I love all things lunar) and said he couldn't wait to see me when I was back. Julian said he'd be on the edge of his seat waiting for my Iceland pictures. I spent the first many days in Europe feeling optimistic about my romantic prospects. Despite all the work I'd done to feel whole on my own, it felt undeniably luxurious to have such promising men within my reach. Men who wanted me to share my travels with them. Men who wanted me when I got home. Men who *cared.*

My optimism soon waned though, as I felt both Julian and Brett pull away. I delivered Julian his birthday poem over an abbreviated FaceTime call on his birthday. He seemed grateful but wasn't able to talk for very long. After that call, I didn't hear from him for over a week. I sent Brett a couple of awesome photos from Iceland and Amsterdam as well as one, like, *really* cute selfie. He didn't respond. I felt crushed and stupid. I'd trained myself not to get excited about men until it was clear they reciprocated in a significant way, and here I was feeling like a stepped-on soda can because of two men I was nowhere near being in a relationship with. Meanwhile, the friends I came to Europe with had daily video calls with their respective boyfriends while I sat nearby drinking wine and scrolling through Instagram to distract myself. I hadn't felt it in a while, but that sinking forever-alone feeling started to spread through me again like blackness.

When I got home, I texted Brett letting him know I was back and available for the date we'd loosely set up before I left. He sent a vague *"let me check my schedule"* reply. Then a day later, he sent a two-minute video ending things with me (yes, an actual video of himself...men in their 40s are something else). He explained that he'd just "lost the spark" and he didn't know why and he was sorry. I didn't understand; all that had happened since we last saw each other was that I went on a two-week vacation. In that same week, Julian and I had another video date and I finally decided to ask if he was still planning another trip to visit me. I watched a combination of sadness and guilt flash across his eyes and I knew immediately: it was over between us. He launched into a long-winded explanation that he didn't know what he wanted to do with his life, and didn't feel like he was going to move to the Bay Area, and he didn't want to do long-distance, and maybe he should have told me all of this sooner. We ended the call cordially and I collapsed teary-eyed into my bed. Alone. Again.

I soon realized that, because of their age, I had higher expectations of Brett and Julian than other (younger) guys I dated. So, when each of them ended things with a same-shit-as-it-ever-was reason, I felt doubly disappointed. And bitter. *Lost "the spark" because he didn't see me for two weeks?! Doesn't know what he wants in life?! At 41?! WHEN DOES IT GET BETTER?!* I was exasperated by the sobering realization that dating older men was not going to magically fix all my dating woes. I felt even worse than before, because after "trying older men" I had no more new dating strategies up my sleeve.

Dating apps had once again done that corrosive thing that they do: inspire hope with the illusion of abundant options, only to have said options vanish into nothingness overnight. I felt the loneliness creeping back in like a sinister fog, heavier than ever before. What the fuck was the point of all of this? Was my life just going to be a maddening carousel of mean-ingless dates forever? I couldn't help comparing myself to my friends, who were almost all in relationships. Meanwhile, I was in a toxic situationship with Hinge, Bumble, and Tinder and each was going *nowhere*. If there was a higher power, I was seething angry at it. I spent the next few months despon-dent and circling dangerously around rock bottom.

CHAPTER TWENTY-NINE

The Extreme Oversharer

We matched on OKCupid after apparently matching on two other apps over the course of a year or so. I only know this because as soon as we matched on OKCupid, The Oversharer immediately messaged me to let me know he was so happy we were *finally* getting a chance to talk. Slight thirst aside, I found his vulnerability and forthcoming nature charming (probably because my standards were on the floor at this point).

That was until he asked after a few messages, "Can I be honest with you?"

I couldn't imagine what this man I hardly knew wanted to be "honest" about, but my curiosity got the best of me. I said, "Yes of course!"

I watched the typing bubbles show up on the screen and stay there for a long, long time. Twenty or so minutes later, I saw why: he sent me a dissertation on a variety of unsavory subjects including how "extremely horny" he was in the mornings, how much he valued connecting with a woman sexually (with graphic details of why), and how uncontrollably attracted he was to me (with descriptions of my various body parts he found sexy). The more of the message I read, the more disgusted I became. By the time I reached the end, I was actually angry at how someone could *ever* think any of this was appropriate to say to a woman you've never met in person. He ended the dissertation with this:

"When you messaged me at 7am, which was very welcomed, as I'd already been up for a while, I had a strong internal groan along the lines of, 'ARRGGHHHH CAN ME AND THIS WOMAN BE FUCKING ALREADYYYYY'"

I replied and told him how inappropriate his message was and that he'd completely creeped me out; I tried to be kind in my explanation, hoping perhaps I could set him straight for the next woman. He was legitimately surprised and then extremely embarrassed. He apologized profusely and said he was just so excited to talk to me after matching those other times. Then he tried to ask me on a date and called me "bro." Obviously, this was the lostest of causes, but what an interesting case study: in this guy's mind, the Venn diagram of "people I call bro" and "women I desperately want to have sex with" seemed to have considerable overlap.

Let this be a cautionary tale: if a man who only knows you from your dating profile asks if he can "be honest" with you, beware! You may be in for an unprompted horny soliloquy.

CHAPTER THIRTY

The Tinder Guy Who Was Either Anomalously Bad at Time Management or Secretly in a Relationship

For some ungodly reason, I still clung to the belief that I might be able to meet my future husband on Tinder. I won't bore you with the details of how I got entangled with My Next Husband Candidate™ on Tinder, but just know his name was Robert, he was brunette (obviously), and he was *very* generous with compliments. In other words, candy to a baby (it's me; I'm the baby).

After the recent disappointments with Julian and others, I let myself *really* bask in Robert's praise, like a high school girl who just posted on hotornot.com and was finding out for the first time that she's "hot." But after a few days of nonstop messaging and compliments, Robert had not yet asked me on a date. There was only so much gushing over the app I could take before meeting someone in person, so I playfully prodded him about it. (I prefer to be asked out rather than do the asking, sue me.) He eventually set up a date the following week and, in the meantime, continued his onslaught of praise; he claimed I was the "perfect woman" who was practically "engineered in a lab" for him. He said he was pretty sure he found what he was looking for and that he'd already deleted his Tinder profile. (Yes, this was eerily familiar to Fake-Marriage Zach. Yes, I continued forward anyway. No, it was not a good idea this time either. Also, is there a "How to Charm Women" manual somewhere that instructs men to use this ridiculous "engineered in a lab" phrase?)

On our first date, Robert took me to a romantic restaurant by the beach, where we sat by a crackling fireplace lined with Christmas lights. We shared a bottle of wine and he opened up about how he was close with his dad but not with his mom. During our sharing of stories about our families, he kept smiling at me with goo-goo eyes and saying how beautiful I looked under the glow of the Christmas lights. He admitted to being nervous to meet me, which immediately made me feel like I could trust him. *So vulnerable!* I was so infatuated that I didn't even mind that he had to take a phone call during dinner. It was work, he said. He managed a team and sometimes had to work late or take unexpected calls. I thought nothing of it at the time.

After our amazing first date, Robert was the perfect gentleman: he drove me home, passionately kissed me goodbye, and asked when he could see me again. It was almost Christmas, so our only option to see each other was the upcoming weekend before we both went home to family. We agreed on Saturday and kissed goodbye. In the days before our next date, Robert was suspiciously absent. He'd send me texts now and then but nowhere near the same volume as before. We both agreed that we liked phone calls, but he never seemed to be able to call when he said he would. He said he was just busy with work, and I knew I had a predilection to anxiety, so I told myself to relax.

The day before our planned second date, Robert told me that he was sick and would have to reschedule our date. He said he didn't want to get me sick and that maybe we could try for Sunday if he was feeling better. He didn't follow up on Sunday so I texted and asked if he was feeling okay. He replied many hours later and said he was still feeling bad but hoped he could see me "soon." When I asked what day would work, we agreed on the 27th, but he had vague plans to go on a fishing trip with his buddies and said he'd get back to me to confirm.

As Christmas approached, he never got back to me about his fishing plans but sent me at least a once-daily text or selfie to butter me up:

I can't wait to kiss you again. I'm going to give you a thousand kisses!!

I've been thinking about you constantly.

I can't stop looking at your pictures, you are so gorgeous Miss Lauren.

I hope it's not weird to say but I miss you.

On Christmas day, he sent a brief Merry Christmas text at 8 a.m. and then was absent until noon the next day. I was trying to be patient, but the uncertainty about our plans was driving me crazy. I asked if he could call me at some point on the 26th so we could solidify our (alleged) plans for the next day, since I was at my parents' house for the holidays (a two-hour drive away from him). He continued to not reply, so I tried calling him in the evening. No answer.

He finally replied around 8 p.m.: **Sorry Lauren, I haven't paid much attention to my phone today, should I call you back?** I was in an anxiety spiral at this point—I'd spent at least half of the evening curled up on the carpet crying to my mom and sister about *"Why is dating so impossible?!?!"*—but I replied kindly that yes, I'd love for him to call me back. He said he'd call on his way home after he stopped off at a buddy's house. He never called. Instead, he texted around 10:30 p.m.: **Hey you, just getting home and I'm a bit beat. Can I give you a call tomorrow?** I was beyond frustrated and couldn't understand why he wouldn't just give me a quick call to confirm plans. I started to feel suspicious. All of this seemed a little too...weird.

The next morning he told me that his sister (who he'd been with) was feeling sick with the same symptoms he had, and he was—yet again—worried about getting me sick. *IS THIS GUY FOR REAL RIGHT NOW?!* I bit back my feelings, which were quickly shifting from anxiety to rage, and once again asked him nicely to call me. He *finally* called and, much to my surprise, he said he was still planning on coming to see me. My anger and anxiety subsided but I still felt incredulous. *I'll believe it when I see it.*

He did actually show up a few hours later and we proceeded to have an amazing all-day and all-night date. I took him to my favorite hidden river oasis in the redwoods and then we shared wine over dinner (where we very randomly ran into Low-Key Soulmate...more on that later). He, once again, was a perfect gentleman and even mentioned that he couldn't wait to make me his girlfriend. We had hours of deep conversation, playful flirting, and constant sexual tension building. All of my suspicions melted away. *I guess he really was just sick and busy with family. I assumed the worst of this guy who is so sweet!*

Robert left early the next morning, saying he needed to help his dad clean his garage. In the following days, he sent lots of *thinking-of-you-you're-so-amazing-wow* texts. I was secretly hoping he'd ask to hang out on New Year's Eve, but he seemed to be tied up spending time with his sister, being hungover, and somehow interviewing for a job? *On December 31st? Hmm.* At this point, it's probably clear that I am an overly-trusting person and this dude was bamboozling me, but I really wanted to believe him! Each thing he said, by itself, was believable. I hadn't yet let myself put the whole picture together. It's honestly wild what you will look past when you're mired in an anxious-avoidant trap and mesmerized by the devil dick. I didn't understand it then but I was completely hooked on his slow drip of intermittent affection—that is, providing unpredictable doses of attention and affection, mixed in with periods of unexplained silence and pull-away.

At the time, I blamed myself for how irrational it made me feel, but I later learned that intermittent affection is *incredibly addictive* on a brain-chemistry level and predictably leads to obsession.

In the following week, more and more excuses kept flooding out. We made plans a week in advance to see each other on the Friday after New Year's and I offered to come to him since he'd been driving a lot for work. He claimed his brother was staying with him for a few days, and asked if we could do his place another weekend instead (I had never been over to his place). Then he said we'd have to push our date to Saturday because one of his employees had COVID and he'd have to cover for him Friday. *Okay, something is definitely sketchy here.*

I began to piece together all the evidence in my head like some sort of crazed detective who finally had enough clues: he deleted his Tinder immediately upon meeting me. He had zero social media or internet presence. He could only ever meet or talk on weekdays; on weekends he went dark. He could never pick up the phone when I called, nor call me back without a lot of delay. He never invited me over to his place. He constantly had nebulous plans and therefore couldn't commit to dates with me. I even checked the metadata on a few selfies and videos he sent me (that he claimed were just for me) and saw that they were taken before we met. It all finally hit me. *THIS DUDE IS TOTALLY PLAYING ME!* I realized that either he truly had the worst luck and time management skills on the planet (doubtful), or that he *must* be in another relationship (more likely). Listen, as the reader you probably realized this paragraphs ago, so you can imagine how stupid I felt when I finally put it all together.

Unsurprisingly, he canceled our plans for Saturday. Even then, I knew this was coming. No way was he going to *actually* see me on a weekend! After my embarrassingly-late detective work conclusion, I was done with this douche-nozzle but I was still pissed and wanted to see what fake bullshit he'd try next. Saturday morning he sent me a three-paragraph text explaining how he wasn't ready to start a new relationship because of work stress, but that I was amazing, and he felt terrible and was so sorry, and a bunch of other placating garbage. *Barf.* He did offer to talk on the phone later and I figured this would be my chance to tell him what a real piece of shit he was, so I took him up on his offer.

In true Robert fashion, he finally called me nine hours later. He sounded exhausted and truly apologetic. To this day I'll never know if his exhaustion was from work or from his other partner who, I had to imagine, he was also pissing off with his incompetence. Anyway, I got straight to the point and let him know that his hot and cold actions had caused me a ton of anxiety and that, if I was being honest, it seemed like he might already be in a relationship. He took this all in stride and only continued to be calm, self-deprecating, and apologetic. (As I'm writing this, I'm realizing he may never have actually *denied* my allegations). I didn't want to sink any more of my energy into this dumpster fire of a man, so we ended the call cordially and I figured we'd never talk again.

But in the following days, he continued to send me "good morning gorgeous" texts, selfies, and comments about my presumed underwear color (why is this a thing?). He said he'd been thinking of me and was clearly fishing for a flirty reply. I finally replied: **you sure are thinking of me a lot lately aren't you?** He never texted me again. Part of me hoped he took a long drive off a short pier or something.

Robert was the final straw: I deleted all my dating apps.

CHAPTER THIRTY-ONE

The Sobriety

There were so many reasons why I'd quit dating apps before. There was the rage-quitting. There was the despair-quitting. There was the quitting because I read that "trying less" would help me manifest my soulmate. There was the quitting because someone else told me to. There was the quitting because the guys I was really interested in didn't message me, or even match with me. There was the quitting because one man disappointed me so deeply that I gave up on dating. There was the quitting because I'd repeatedly run out of people to swipe on and it made me feel inexplicably pathetic, desperate, and alone.

There were so many reasons why I'd quit alcohol before too. There was the quitting because it would help me stay skinny. There was the quitting because my boyfriend didn't like it. There was the quitting because my parent was an alcoholic. There was the quitting because of the red-hot shame and nausea I felt after a night of binge drinking. There was the quitting because my energy healer told me to. There was the quitting because I thought some universal power up in the ether was judging me and would only grant me a boy-friend once I got sober. There was the quitting to simply prove to myself that I could stop, for a while.

None of those times I quit ever stuck, for dating apps or for alcohol. Mostly because my reasons were to *get* something, or because my impetus came from someone else. But something about this time felt...different. There is a certain resolve that comes after finding yourself, at 32 years old, sobbing to your mom and younger sisters about yet another problematic man from the internet. There is a certain *oh god, something REALLY needs to change* feeling when you finally admit to yourself that mostly you drink because you feel so achingly lonely. It had always been easy to blame the men before. For the loneliness. For my quarterly bouts of despair. For the hopeless, hungover Sunday mornings. It felt justified to toss them into boxes: *Fuckboy! Emotionally unavailable! No chemistry! Peter Pan! Piece-of-shit ghoster!* And yeah, that felt good for a while; to sift through the details of these failed relation-ships or situationships with my friends and nail these men to the wall with our (often justified) excoriations. But for what? What was I really getting out of all of this except inci-dentally developing an insidious hatred toward men? What was I getting out of this lifestyle of cycling through my five dating apps every day, breaking only to go out drinking on Saturday nights with the ever-diminishing hope of meeting a guy out in the real world?

I was finally ready to let go. Of the chance of finding love on Hinge or Bumble or Tinder or The League (barf) or any of the other fringe apps I downloaded out of desperation. Of the sick satisfaction that hating on men with friends brought me (even if some of those men *did* suck). Of the comfort that four glasses of red wine brought me. Of the notion that I would somehow miss out on the love of my life if I wasn't on every app possible *and* out every weekend looking hot and available. I was finally ready to heed my inner knowing, which had been whispering to me for some time now that there was a lot of life waiting for me beyond the clutches of alcohol. And in a more subtle way, that there was a lot of freedom (and even magic) to be had if I could release my white-knuckled grip on finding a partner—a grip I'd had since I was 15 years old when my first boyfriend (who I didn't even like that much) broke up with me to date my friend.

This chapter isn't about glorifying sobriety—not really. It's about choosing what works for *you* even and *especially* when it's not what everyone else is doing. I held onto both alcohol and dating apps for a *long* time because it was what everyone around me was doing. I didn't want to have to explain myself. And trust me, *everyone* asks "Why?" when you're not drinking. Or when you're just single and not actively dating. My reasoning felt murky and complicated, even to me, so there was no way I was going to be able to explain my choices well to others. *I'm not drinking tonight. Why? Oh, I guess because I've been worried for years that I have a minor drinking problem because alcoholism runs in my family, and I don't think it's a big deal but I feel depressed for two to five days after most times I drink, so I'm just not drinking. Electively. For a while. But I'm not an alcoholic!* Yeah, try barking that into some acquaintance's ear at a loud bar.

I watched alcohol-soaked nights unfold in front of me for years and wrapped myself in an ever-tightening straight jacket of "shoulds." Because everyone around me drank. Everywhere I went, drinking was not only normalized, it was encouraged. Come to think of it, it was not only encouraged but practically mandated—if you didn't drink in a social environment, you were *lameeee* and boring. In a professional environment, drinking was how you got in with the higher-ups and slithered your way into the elusive boys' club. Choosing not to drink often meant that you missed out on invisible benefits, the type that come from the boozy chumming with execs past 10 p.m. when the corporate hierarchy magically flattens.

Thus my internal narrative about alcohol became a tyrannical parade of shoulds: *Everyone here is getting drunk and no one is batting an eye, I should just be normal and order another one. See? She's drinking more than me, I should stop worrying. I should only have three drinks tonight to prove I can moderate. I just spent a long day at work and really just want to go home, but my team keeps saying "just come for one, the CEO is buying" so I guess I should suck it up and go. I feel kinda bored/lonely/hopeless, I should drink more to have as much fun as everyone else.* I'd justify my own drinking by comparing it to someone who drank more. I'd (silently) blame situations or certain people for encouraging me to drink. I'd oscillate between practically chugging a bottle of wine to make my Saturday more fun, or not drinking at all in an act of defiance, to *prove* I had control over alcohol.

After years of trying to find balance, I eventually got better at owning and explaining my choices with alcohol. I implemented an annual sober January that I felt proud of. But I still felt...undefined. In a society where "addict" and "alcoholic" were well-defined labels, what was I? What is the word or label or category for when you have a problem but it's not alcoholism or full-on love addiction? Where do you go for support when you feel like an imposter in 12-step groups but everyone you know drinks and seems to date without issue? I realized that I had to start defining my own truths:

Truth number one: I am not an alcoholic but I do have a drinking problem.

Truth number two: I am not a love addict but I do struggle with dating and addictive behavior patterns.

Truth number three: it's not the alcohol or the dating apps themselves that are the problem—plenty of people use each without issue—it's *my* relationship with each that is problematic.

This last truth was particularly important to land on because it afforded me the motivation to take personal responsibility for these problematic "relationships" without any adulterating justification or blame. I had built a cage around myself by externalizing alcohol and apps as if they were some sinister force happening *to* me. To make real change, I had to put the power fully back into my own hands. Either I could keep feeling like shit, knowing full well I was the one in the driver's seat who kept circling through Shitville and convincing myself I could figure out how to like it there, or I could make a change. So, come January 2022, I decided to quit the two biggest detractors from my happiness: dating apps and alcohol.

CHAPTER THIRTY-TWO

The Low-Key Soulmate—Part IV

After the sky-raining-fire fiasco at Burning Man, I kept Miles blocked for over a year. It served the purpose I'd hoped for; I finally had the time and space to grieve him properly without the scab being ripped open by a surprise text. During this time I journaled extensively and dug into *why* I'd been so stuck on him. The answer that eventually emerged was simple: he made me feel seen in a way no other partner had. Being around him had unearthed this playful, uninhibited side of myself that I'd never known before. By introducing me to things like backpacking and Burning Man, he'd incidentally brought me closer to what made my soul feel most alive: nature, play, curiosity, creativity, and presence. I realized these were all values *I* could embody on my own. I realized I hadn't been really stuck on *him*. Instead, I was stuck on the incorrect belief that only *he* held the power to bring out my true self. But no one else held that power, it was mine and mine alone!

After this realization, the anger and resentment toward Miles slowly seeped out of my body and I was left with a kind of melancholy nostalgia. He'd impacted my life in a lot of meaningful ways and I felt grateful. Outside of a romantic context, I missed him as a person, but I knew it was unlikely we could ever be close again. Nevertheless, after healing enough to where I didn't *need* anything from him, I unblocked him and sent him a text:

Hi *caterpillar emoji* do you want to be friends?

I was tired of carrying the burden of his ghost in my head. Somehow the forced silence between us felt like it had become dangerously fertile ground for my imagination. I figured talking to the real him would be grounding. And it was. He replied:

If we crossed paths in person I was planning to give you a half shove and ask "if we're still not talking forever," so yes

I laughed and felt instantly at ease. We caught up over text about our various pandemic journeys and then the conversation naturally petered out. Almost a year went by without more contact. During this time, I dreamed about Miles often—at least every other night. It wasn't like I was thinking about him before bed or anything, but he was a constant figure in my dreams. It was very confusing; I'd spent *so* much time and effort getting over him but my subconscious kept spitting him up at night, forcing me to spend time with him in bizarro, jumbled scenes. I wanted nothing more than to just be done with this saga. It had been over three years since we last hooked up and I felt pathetic for still dreaming about him. Was he even thinking about me at all? I'd tell myself *No! Of course not!* to try and bully my subconscious into moving on.

Concurrently, I continued to delve deeper into spirituality and connecting with my inner self. I figured if the regular world didn't have any answers for me, maybe the spiritual world did. I booked a session with a woman whose book I read about connecting with your soul. I really resonated with the concept that we (humans) have the answers we seek within us. During the session, I asked her about Miles, explaining how we had this seemingly unbreakable soul connection (at least on my end, but I suspected maybe on his too). She guided me through asking my soul about it. Then, after the session when I sat quietly and inquired inward about what to do, I got *very* surprising, clear guidance: reach out to Miles on August 25th (a few weeks from that day). I *never* received internal guidance like this, it was usually much more vague. I was still on the fence about believing in all this stuff, but I figured I had exhausted every other method, so embracing the "woo-woo" and listening to "my soul" for once couldn't hurt.

As August 25th approached, I got cold feet. *Why would I do this? I don't want to open another can of worms.* I pushed it out of my mind and focused on my upcoming travel plans. But then! On the 24th, I was on my Vespa going across town and some heavy traffic on my regular route forced me to take a side street, where I drove right past Miles. He was running and didn't see me but I rode in wide-eyed disbelief all the way to my destination. *What are the chances?!?! Today of all days?!* Maybe there was something to this inner guidance stuff. I had my answer: I decided to text him the next day.

Within a few texts, Miles let me know that he'd recently moved in with his girlfriend. *Ooof.* I hated to admit it, but swallowing that news felt sharply unpleasant. The specific loneliness of realizing someone you once loved has moved on prickled against my insides. I didn't let my discomfort show to him though, and politely congratulated him on this life milestone like any friend would. Meanwhile, I was *extremely* single and listening to "spiritual guidance" to text my ex-situationship who clearly had moved on in a *very* tangible way. I felt like an idiot. And lost. Why had I been so clearly guided to do this? *Yeah, funny joke—fuck you too, soul.*

Thankfully, after a week of digesting this information, I felt much better and understood that I needed to receive this news to complete the next step of my moving-on process. It actually did feel like a gift of unexpected closure that had been bestowed upon me—the tiny sliver of hope about Miles and I ending up together that had stubbornly barnacled onto my heart could finally be chipped off.

Yet, for unexplained maybe-cosmic reasons, I continued to run into him. In the ensuing four months, I ran into him *three* more times. Before this, I had not seen him in over two years so it was jarring, to say the least. The most jarring time was the last time, over Christmas break when I was visiting my hometown of Santa Cruz and on a date with probably-in-another-relationship Robert. I was two bites into my pepperoni pizza when Miles and his girlfriend walked right by our table. *Seriously? Here?!* Miles and I seemed equally shocked to see each other, especially given that we were hours away from San Francisco, where we both lived. We clumsily introduced our significant (well, in my case, insignificant) others, and I tried my hardest not to show Robert how stunned I was.

"Oh, he's just kind of an...ex...thing," I said, flippantly, focusing on my pizza and avoiding eye contact at all costs. I had never asked the word "thing" to do more work.

After that encounter, I felt like the Universe *must* be trying to tell me something. I cannot overstate how much I am into hard evidence and science, but all of this with Miles was a little *too* weird. Call it anomalous or random chance or serendipity, but I'd never experienced this level of coincidence before, with anyone or anything. About a month after Christmas, I texted Miles and asked if he wanted to meet up, on *purpose*, because it felt like we still had something...unresolved between us. He agreed and joked about how talking under "not a fire-raining sky" might be healing for both of us. We agreed in a low-pressure way to meet sometime within the upcoming year.

We met up on an overcast November afternoon in 2022, for the first time (intentionally) since 2017. That same familiarity between us was as present as ever; we knew the five-year-ago versions of each other really well, but a *lot* had changed. I'd heard through mutual friends that he'd recently gotten engaged and I congratulated him on it. After trading a few more life milestones, we reflected on our tumultuous past. With time and space, we could both admit that the addictive push-pull nature of our relationship had kept us stuck on each other. We'd separately struggled with addictive dating behaviors and had to learn how to untangle the addiction from the person. We'd both chased those transient highs and saw the wreckage that ensued. I explained to him that he was a huge catalyst in my personal growth journey and I was super grateful for our time together. He reciprocated and we talked about a few of our favorite memories together.

It was a strange feeling sharing that same 10-foot radius again with the person I once wanted more than anything. But it was necessarily platonic between us, now, forever. I still wasn't completely sure what had been "love" between us and what was an attachment borne from the addictive push-pull, and it sounded like he wasn't sure either. I'd long exhausted that topic in my mind and wasn't interested in giving it a stage. But like any well-worn habit, the underlying question bubbled to the surface like it had thousands of times before: *I wonder if he still has any feelings for me?* I laughed at myself for it. *A guy can literally be about to get married and you'll still wonder if he thinks about you!* I easily let the thought float away. It didn't hold any meaning for me anymore; it was just a vestige of the past, a crutch from that still-healing self who thought she needed Miles to breathe.

If those years of meditation and therapy taught me anything, it was that your old selves—that is, your old habits, thoughts, feelings, and beliefs—still live inside you and occasionally make a clamoring attempt at grabbing the steering wheel. I had learned how to give those old parts of me a voice, to pour the old feelings onto pages and paintings, but ultimately not act on, or define myself by them. As we neared the end of our walk, I felt inside for my current self—the stable 32-year-old—and I found a calm equanimity toward Miles. No sadness, no wanting, no resentment. *I think this is what being truly over someone feels like!*

After all the years of chaos and pining, the neutrality felt almost suspicious. I realized I had never felt it before. I had always gotten over people by getting into another relationship, or by distracting myself with drunken nights out, or by shoving my feelings down and pretending I could move on that way. This, with Miles, was the first time I had undertaken the painstaking process of getting over someone by turning inward, facing the darkness, and allowing it to take as long as it would take. It had taken a long time. A *long* time. (Three years? Who's counting? I definitely was. Damn you, data-brain.) But the unshakeable faith I had in myself now was *so* worth it. I had *finally* broken the cycle of un-attaching my pain from one man and attaching it to another. For the first time in a decade, I felt immutably free. There it was again: closure. Impolitely late, as usual.

In the end, despite some maybe-cosmic force relentlessly throwing us toward each other, it wasn't meant to be between Miles and me. We weren't soulmates in the live-happily-ever-after kind of way. I do, however, still attest that we were soulmates of a different kind: the kind where you crash into each other and break open, spilling your precious contents all over the ground and your only way forward is to clumsily gather yourself back up and try to fit everything back inside. But you don't fit anymore, into that old shape, and you don't really know why because it all fit before. Nevertheless, you have to become whole again, so you break some pieces into smaller pieces and you glue other pieces together and you assemble and by the time you're done you're altogether different but somehow more beautiful. You're kintsugi[14] in human form. You are the same you but with golden veins, showing where you found a way to heal (even though you really would have rather *not* at the start of all of this). You are the same you but with cracks, necessary cracks, to let your soul shine through.

In the end, I learned there is priceless wisdom in ephemerality. Sometimes a person staying for only a few seasons teaches you more than if they were to stick around forever. Sometimes a person comes into your life to completely transform you, and part of that process is the transformation that happens when they leave you. Sometimes the parts of yourself that you unearth after someone leaves are worth the pain of their leaving. In hindsight, you may even realize how that person leaving was the best thing that ever happened to you. And maybe you'll even see how sometimes there are no villains in an ephemeral love story, just people. People who are endearingly flawed, doing their best to contend with their frustrating and unrelenting humanness. People with lonely, hungry hearts that simply ache to be *known*.

Lastly, I learned that when it comes to love, mostly the end of the journey looks nothing like you expected. Sometimes you don't end up with that person you once wanted so badly, and *that* is the blessing.

---

14   kintsugi (noun): the Japanese art of repairing broken pottery by mending the areas of breakage with lacquer dusted or mixed with powdered gold, silver, or platinum. As a philosophy, it treats breakage and repair as part of the history of an object, rather than something to disguise.

CHAPTER THIRTY-THREE
The Unexpected Reddit Guy

After a few months free from alcohol and dating apps, I felt indescribably wonderful. I know, *I know*, barf, so cliche— woman sticks with new, healthy habits for an unimpressive amount of time and then won't shut up about how *great and different* she feels—but it's important for the story, so let me have this one. I felt like a balloon finally released from its weight and allowed to fly. I felt shiny and confident and bursting with creative energy. Most of all, I felt free.

I wasn't going on dates and, besides my almost-daily trips to cafes to write, I wasn't putting myself in places to be "seen." It felt *so* good to just let *go* of trying to meticulously control my love life, for once. I still had that fearful voice come up sometimes—*What if you never find anyone?*—but I'd reached a point of trust in myself, and in the mysterious ways of the world, that my hope was consistently out-voicing my fear. I guess you could even say I had cultivated my belief in magic.

During this time, a slew of previous dating app matches started popping up like whack-a-moles. Some through texts (normal), one through a random alternate texting app (weird), and one through Google Chat (weird, and also kind of funny). The Google Chat guy had matched with me five to six months prior, showered me with compliments, said he'd *love* to take me on a picnic, and then blocked me in the middle of planning said picnic date. So yeah, whatever the diametric opposite of interested is, I was that when he popped back up again. But my curiosity got the best of me and I asked why he ghosted and blocked me. He deflected (shocker) and then started delving into an extreme overshare about his adolescent erectile dysfunction issues and how he'd overcome them with tantric sex. *What the fuck is it with men and inappropriately oversharing to women they don't even know?*

I told him to maybe look into help other than women over Google Chat and then went to my favorite place to post about and discuss this "oversharing phenomenon": Reddit. I was a frequent reader and commenter on a subreddit called Dating Over Thirty because I found a lot of solace and sanity in commiserating about dating struggles with internet strangers. My post quickly gained a lot of popularity and started some interesting discourse about oversharing and boundaries in dating. Then I received a couple of private messages related to the post that would completely alter the course of my life.

One was from a guy in Texas who thought my dating stories were funny and asked if I had any more. "DO I EVER," I told him and linked my Medium page where I had written about some of my more ridiculous dating encounters. To my complete surprise and delight, he said he'd already come across my writing organically a couple of months prior and really enjoyed it.

"You should write a book!" he insisted.

I gave him the answer I gave to anyone (including myself) when I heard this suggestion: "I knowww, I want to, but I don't know what it would be about."

He persisted and told me to just write an outline. Just put something on paper! And for some reason, I listened to this random stranger. It was the tiniest little nudge that I needed. After a few days and an unexplainable dose of serendipity, I had a book outline, an amazing book editor, and the warmest ball of joy spreading through me.

The second message was from a guy who had left a thoughtful comment about boundaries on my post. His message was unassuming and kind, explaining that he'd been following my post and liked what I had to say. He seemed to have no agenda and ended the message by wishing me luck in my dating life. I was intrigued by this polite internet man who *wasn't* sliding into my inbox to hit on me. After a few messages back and forth, we realized that we lived only a few miles away from each other, which is a bit miraculous in itself because Reddit is global. He told me his name (Ethan) and admitted he was actually only 29, but liked lurking in the Dating Over Thirty subreddit. After several paragraphs-long messages between us, he asked me out for coffee. He did this without knowing what I looked like (most people on Reddit don't have profile photos). He sent a selfie with the invitation to prove he wasn't some catfish creep. He was cute! I figured *why not?* and met up with him the following morning.

As I walked into the cafe, I immediately spotted him in the back corner wearing a red flannel and reading a book. He stood up once he saw me and flashed me a warm smile. *Oh. Oh, wow. He is handsome and looks like he gives amazing hugs!* He wrapped me in a tight hug and we sat down to chat. I subtly studied him from across the table. He had these kind, honey-brown eyes that said, *"I probably do favors for strangers because of who I am as a person."* His neck tinged slightly red as we talked; nerves, probably. I was endeared. He was a welcome change from the jaded, well-practiced dating population I was used to.

It didn't take long for me to gather that he was close with his family and the thoughtful, caretaker type. He worked for the local public library system, which I found wholesome and fitting. He was charming but not in the sugary way so many other guys had been; he showed interest by actively listening, asking curious questions, and giving me a few sincere compliments. By the end of the date, it was clear there was mutual interest and he asked if he could take me out again soon. I easily said yes. I left the date feeling simply happy and, notably, *not* manically excited. Not *oh my god, I just met my husband.* Not *holy bejesus, we have insane chemistry.* Not *I will be anxiously waiting for a text from him.* Just happy. And mildly optimistic. He texted me an hour after the date letting me know he had a great time and couldn't wait to take me out again.

He planned the second date of my dreams—a short, scenic hike and brunch reservations at a restaurant overlooking the San Francisco Bay (men who make reservations—so hot).

After brunch we both wanted to keep hanging out, so he took me to get ice cream. He got excited when he saw they had blue ice cream and ordered it with an 11-year-old-boy fervor. When we went to sit on a bench overlooking the ocean, I giggled and told him his whole mouth was blue. His cheeks flushed and in that moment we both could feel the palpable tension that hangs before a first kiss. He leaned in to kiss me and thus began the start of *us*, a relationship founded on blue lips.

After that second date, we just never stopped seeing each other. We camped, we ate, we road-tripped, we went to parties together. He took care of me in a way that was completely unfamiliar to me but seemed like the most natural thing in the world to him. He cooked me dinners, stocked his apartment with tampons and my favorite coffee, picked me up for dates even though I totally could have driven myself, walked on the car-side of the sidewalk to keep me safe, and was always generally making sure I was comfortable. Sure, maybe this is basic boyfriend stuff, but for me, being cared for like this felt like being wrapped in a soft warmth that I'd desperately craved but never quite felt before.

Despite how wonderful it felt to be cared for, I also began to develop a conflicting (unfortunately familiar) feeling: avoidance. The Avoidant Line of Questions started bubbling up: *Why does he like me so much? Why is he so nice? This is too easy, am I bored?* That same old belief resurfaced: love too easily won was cheap and not worth having. Something about it felt eerily familiar to what I'd felt all those years prior with Miles. I couldn't believe I was here again. I'd spent the last few years undoing this belief and fixing my "man picker." I'd dreamed of the day when I'd meet a handsome, caring man who would adore me, and yet, when I finally met him, there was a part of me that inexplicably wanted to push him away. I was frustrated, confused, and humbled. In recent years, I'd thought of myself as "aggressively emotionally available," but clearly I still had some work to do.

I wrestled with my avoidance for months, during which I could feel myself observing Ethan, reticent, waiting for him to make a mistake. I had on my metaphorical headlamp, searching high and low for red flags, but I couldn't find any. The worst thing about him was that he preferred Safeway to Trader Joe's. Yet I continued to be on high alert. I kept finding insignificant reasons to doubt him as a partner, like when he picked me up at the airport a few months in and (sweetly) thought I'd want to be greeted on foot and then walk a half mile to the car with him and my suitcase. *Why would I want that? Can I not trust his decision-making?* Or there was the fact that he didn't seem to tire of spending time with me. *Shouldn't he want "space"? Shouldn't he get to know me more before committing so much time to me?* Or there was the fact that he was more introverted and reserved, providing stark contrast to myself and many of my friends. *Shouldn't he have a more active social life? Why isn't he instantly comfortable around all my friends?* I didn't *want* to be doing this—tabulating data about why this perfectly wonderful man might not be right for me—but it didn't even feel like a choice. It felt like a necessary protection mechanism built up over many years of disappointment.

It took me some time to realize that how Ethan was treating me, in both words and actions, was how a person treats someone they're genuinely very into. My baseline for this had become skewed over all the years of app dating; I was so used to the inconsistency and unavailability that was all over the apps that when presented with consistency and availability, it felt almost stifling. The same way sunlight is stifling after spending time in the dark. *What do you mean I don't have to marinate in anxiety about how this person feels about me? What do you mean I don't have to work for his time and attention, it's just freely offered?* No one told me this, but there can be a very real adjustment period after receiving something (or someone) you've always wanted. Good things take time to accept too.

So, although the aforementioned Avoidant Line of Questioning felt convincing and familiar, I had almost a decade of wisdom on my prior self and I chose a new approach this time around: I named my avoidant feelings and talked openly about them to Ethan. I'd spent most of my life ashamed of feeling either extreme of the anxious-avoidant spectrum, but I reminded myself of what I'd learned in my years of healing: shame can't survive in the open. So, I unwrapped my shame and put it on display. I committed to not hiding parts of myself, even if those parts made me feel like I was 23 with commitment issues again.

Thankfully, Ethan was patient and understanding. He didn't push me and gave me space to process my feelings (that were almost certainly a "me thing" and not really about him). It was a little bumpy for a couple of months as I worked through the wave of avoidant feelings and he tried to keep composure about it. There were days I felt unexplainably distant and needed space. He could sense this and it made him feel uneasy and confused. As someone who was usually the anxious one in the relationship, I understood all too well what he was feeling and did my best to reassure him. It was a strange feeling to be in this opposite role, like learning to walk with a suddenly-new pair of feet.

Eventually, the wave passed and I felt myself soften into him. Maybe I needed time to believe he was real and not another man who would promise me the world and then disappoint me. Maybe I never really dealt with my fear of commitment and this was the time for that. I wasn't really sure about the math behind it all, but maybe I didn't need all the analyzing and equations to protect myself anymore. Maybe I could just let it be really good.

After that, it didn't take long for love to arrive. There was a meadow on a camping trip where we both quietly fell in love below the fading sunlight, though neither of us admitted it then. A few weeks later, we sat on a bluff overlooking the Pacific Ocean and he turned to me and said, "Okay, I'm just going to say it first...I love you."

I immediately started crying. The way he purred those words out in his deep voice felt like velvet brushing between my ribs and cradling my heart. Those same words had been pushing against my teeth for some time. It had been six years since I'd said them to a romantic partner.

"I love you," I said back between tears and a gigantic smile.

♡ ♡ ♡

When I sat down to write this book, I was single. I'd been online/app dating since I was 22 and had been on over 200 dates, so I had *more* than enough content for a book about modern dating. It felt especially notable that I'd never actually found a serious relationship through online dating. All I had to show from a decade of high-volume dating was a smattering of transient one- to three-month connections. It felt important to write about *that* reality—the one without the prototypical "happily ever after" ending. I wanted to write a story where self-grown freedom, peace, and happiness were enough of a happy ending in and of themselves.

Then, suddenly, I was no longer single. But I was *committed* to this not changing me too much! I found it annoying when people would get into relationships and become less "fun," or worse, disappear altogether. I didn't want to become a cliche. I wanted to somehow remain loyal to the fiercely independent self that I'd cultivated over the past six years. She'd worked *tirelessly* to depend only on herself for validation, comfort, and happiness. In a way, it felt like letting myself lean on a partner for these things was forfeiting all of that hard work, as if enjoying and thriving in partnership somehow invalidated who I'd proudly grown into while single.

But slowly, as I settled into being in a stable, committed partnership, I realized that my changing was inevitable (and was a good thing). Just as the years of feeling anxious in unstable "relationships" had tugged me away from my center, being in a healthy, secure relationship was giving me the space to become *more* myself. Despite how much I didn't want to admit it at first, receiving regular validation and care from a partner was incredibly healing (this is obviously not a hot take, but it was a novel feeling for me after those six chaotic years of dating). I felt my remaining body-image issues melt away. I felt my urge to binge eat—which I'd battled with since high school—completely disappear. I felt my creative energy blossom like never before. A deep sense of relief washed over me, the kind that comes from being seen, accepted, and loved for exactly who you are. I finally realized that my extensive struggles with dating, my repeated mistakes, my always-long grieving process, my not-petite body, my collapsing into a sobbing heap over a Tinder guy even at 32 years old—none of it ever meant I was unworthy of love. I always "knew" this in theory, but there's a difference to really *feeling* worthy, deeply, in your soul. I finally understood that there was nothing "wrong" with me all along, I just hadn't met the right person yet.

I'd always heard that you shouldn't *need* a partner because a relationship should be the cherry on top of an already fulfilling life. But using this adage as a north star, in my opinion, is a double-edged sword. It encourages us to create our own happiness (the good part), but it also quietly implies that we can somehow "turn off" our need for companionship (the unrealistic part). For many people, including myself, the idea of reaching 100% fulfillment, healing, and contentedness while single feels like chasing an impossible goal. After chasing this impossible goal for most of my adult life, I find it important to present an alternate stance: you do not need to be fully healed, fulfilled, or content with being single to find love. Yes, of course, build a life that brings you joy and purpose. Yes, of course, work on your independence and self-love. Yes, of course, foster love through your friendships and family. But also, can we give ourselves permission to loudly and openly desire romantic love and partnership? Can we stop telling single people how they should feel or not feel? Can we allow the yearning for companionship to be a welcomed and expected part of our journey to fulfillment? For so many of us, this is an innate human need, and trying to shut it off is akin to trying to convince yourself you're not hungry—the feeling will go away temporarily but, eventually, it'll pop back up with a vengeance.

I wish someone had told me a decade ago that my aching desire for love was a *good* thing and that I didn't need to dim it down to find a relationship. I wish someone had told me to grow that burning in my chest, to nurture it, to pour it into art and words and dogs and sunrises and everyone around me. I wish someone had told me that it's okay to feel lonely and desperate and bitter about being single sometimes, and that admitting this doesn't make you pathetic (just the opposite, in fact). I wish someone had told me that it would all work out in the end, even if I didn't know where the end was or how to get there. I wish someone had told me that most endings aren't bad, or even endings at all, but rather invitations to become. I wish I knew that I could trust what my heart was telling me all along: you are meant for love. Even if that love isn't permanent. Even if that love takes way longer to arrive than you expected. Even if that love shatters you into pieces so completely that you stop believing in love altogether. You never stop being meant for love, if that is what you want.

I wish someone had told me at the start of all of this that love is mostly unpredictable and impossible to plan for. But also, more importantly, that there is a certain magic within the uncertainty, if you can get past the maddening truth that you don't know the how, the when, or the who. Or if you'll meet in an elevator, or on Hinge, or at that house party you almost didn't go to. Or if you'll be gifted a delightful stranger from the internet who wouldn't have even made it through your dating app age filters. If you can get past not knowing, if you can somehow hold the precarious uncertainty that gnaws at your bones when it's dark out, if you can let time do its mysterious bidding, then you might one day look at your life and realize it turned out better than you could have ever imagined.

If You Could See the Whole Future at Once, Would You Look?

Sometimes I find myself wanting to see the whole future at once. You know? The insatiable urge to binge-watch. Or maybe hungrily read it like a real page-turner novel, gasping and rejoicing and crying for all that's to come.

But I am at least wise enough to know this would be like staring into the sun. Bright and exciting for a short moment, and then quickly corrosive and unrelenting. We aren't made to behold everything there is to know all at once.

Time, in this way, is our greatest gift. The way it drips by like cosmic molasses. Each drop contains a dose of our lives, verdant and teeming even in this most minuscule portion. Maybe in this way, time is actually medicine, delivering in digestible drops the gluttonous richness of living. Drip. Drip. Drip.

A drop of despair here, a drop of awe there. Sprinkles of regret and hope and wonder and exasperation and grief and frustration and elation and boredom. Each drop raining down on us until we are sticky and mired in our lives so completely that we have no choice but to surrender to it all.

So yeah, I want to see the future. I want to peek at it. I want to burn my eyes for a moment just to see what's out there. Don't we all? It's the most human desire in the world to want to understand more than what we are made for. To singe ourselves getting too close to beautiful, bright things.

But as I am reminded by the sun as it meets my morning eyes from behind the cottony puffs in the sky: time keeps us safe by delivering us the too-bright unknown in measure. I'll keep wanting to know the future, no doubt. But for now, I'll be here lapping up the fecund drops one at a time, savoring my life as it's dripped onto my tongue.

Acknowledgements

I have the most wonderful support network and I want to express my gratitude to each and every person who helped me on my writing journey. To my editor, Emily: thank you for helping me believe I had a story worth telling—you were exactly who I needed by my side. To my book designer, Kristy: thank you for going out of your way to create a cover I really love and for your endless patience during the process. To my beta readers, Sky, Hannah, and Melanie: thank you for the invaluable feedback—your advice and encouragement to get on my "soap box" brought out SO much goodness and really transformed so many chapters. To all of my friends who made a point to ask about my book and build me up (you know who you are): thank you, your support means more than you know. To my sis, Anne: thank you for being so excited about my book when I first told you about my idea— you were the final nudge I needed to find an editor and just start writing the book already! To my sis, Jayne: thank you for your wisdom and for all the times you held my heart when I was crying over yet another dating app disappointment. To Dad: you have always made me believe I could do anything and I can never thank you enough for all of the ways you have patiently and lovingly supported me. To Mom: being your daughter has been the greatest blessing of my life—thank you for teaching me resilience and integrity in my most stubborn moments and thank you for being the reason I know what truly selfless love feels like. To my Grumpy: I can't believe how lucky I am to have you, you are more than I could have ever dreamed of—thank you for healing my heart.

LAUREN JOSEPHINE is a bioengineer by education, writer by passion, and redwood tree enthusiast by choice. Her penchant for writing about love, relationships, and grief started with blogging on Tumblr after a devastating breakup at age 19. Lauren grew up near Santa Cruz, California and moved to San Francisco in her mid 20s for a job at a startup, and also because she was pretty sure the dating prospects were better there. Her arduous dating journey in San Francisco eventually inspired her to write a book with one simple goal: helping others feel less alone during their search for love. *Looking for Something Serious* is Lauren's first book.